longing for
enough
in a culture of
more

longing for
enough
in a culture of
more

PAUL L. ESCAMILLA

ABINGDON PRESS / NASHVILLE

LONGING FOR ENOUGH IN A CULTURE OF MORE

Copyright © 2007 by Abingdon Press

This book is printed on acid-free paper.

Library of Congress Cataloging-in-Publication Data

Escamilla, Paul L.
  Longing for enough in a culture of more / Paul L. Escamilla.
     p. cm.
  Includes bibliographical references and index.
  ISBN 978-0-687-46651-1 (pbk. : alk. paper)
  1. Contentment—Religious aspects—Christianity. 2. Satisfaction—Religious aspects—Christianity. I. Title.

BV4647.C7E83 2007
242—dc22

                                                                    2007017848

All scripture quotations unless noted otherwise are taken from the New Revised Standard Version of the Bible, copyright 1989, Division of Christian Education of the National Council of the Churches of Christ in the United States of America. Used by permission. All rights reserved.

Revised Standard Version of the Bible, copyright 1946, 1952, 1971 by the Division of Christian Education of the National Council of the Churches of Christ in the United States of America. Used by permission. All rights reserved.

"Ash Wednesday" by T. S. Eliot from COLLECTED POEMS, 1909–1962; by permission of Harcourt Brace Jovanovich and Faber and Faber Ltd.

Excerpt of speech by Martin Luther King, Jr. reprinted by arrangement with the Heirs to the Estate of Martin Luther King, Jr. c/o Writers House as agent for the proprietor, New York, NY. Copyright 1963 Martin Luther King, Jr., copyright renewed 1991 Corretta Scott King.

"I Did Not Know These Messengers (The One Who Taught Beside the Sea)" by John Thornburg. © 2003 Copyright by Wayne Leupold Editions, Inc. Reprinted by permission.

A study guide for this book, as well as a list of resources,
can be found at www.cokesbury.com/teachablebooks

09 10 11 12 13 14 15 16—10 9 8 7 6

MANUFACTURED IN THE UNITED STATES OF AMERICA

To

James Lisle

and

Zuleme Gragson Delaplain,

and

Elvira Flores

and

Gregorio Escamilla

who, as with durable saints in every time and place,
needed little
and
offered much.

Contents

Part Four *The Good Society*

Part Five *The Good Earth*

Acknowledgments

*W*hat has become of my initial endeavor to write a book is roughly the same unfolding process I remember from my grandparents' summer garden. One person usually planted the sprouting potato, or the beans, or the seed corn, folding them into the soil one solitary spring day under the prospect of rain. Then, over the following weeks and months, others came from out of the blue—children, grandchildren, in-laws, neighbors—to water and weed, mend fence or turn out turtles, pluck the ripe ears from the stalk, twist the reddening tomato from the stem, roll the fatted melon from the vine, dig the nest of potatoes from the dirt, cut the okra, snap the beans. From the seed of one hand's springtime planting came the summer labors of many more, and, from their labors, the harvest.

This book is such an effort, widening over time. Barbara Dorff, Marilyn Oden, Robin Lovin, and my parents, Dorothy and Roberto Escamilla, have been among those who, early on, bent over the seedling and whispered, "Grow! Grow!" In the Abingdon office, Jill Reddig has been present at every step with guidance and support. Alyce McKenzie, John Holbert, Barry Webster, Cy and Nancy Watson, Nancy Roberts, Loren Willet, and John Thornburg read drafts willingly and then spoke constructively. Rhonda Huser nimbly and magnanimously provided source and citation assistance. When I sought a brief retreat for writing, Cedarbrake Retreat Center graciously let me come there, and Spring Valley United Methodist Church generously let me go. Anna Hosemann-Butler, my good partner in the parish work, and her husband Ted Butler, kindly offered a place apart at one critical stage in the project, and that haven of windows, woods, and water fed both the manuscript and the soul. For all of these partners in the garden work, I am deeply grateful. God has given the increase.

The person to whom I owe the ink from every page of this undertaking is my wife, Elizabeth. In the course of this venture, she has supported me through thick and thin, letting me write, write, and write some more, willingly going with me to seek a new candle when the last was beginning to burn low, always believing it worthwhile to do so. Much of what I have seen and wanted to say in writing, she has seen also and helped me to say better than I otherwise might. To you, Elizabeth, more than ink from the page, my heart.

That is something of the "who" in this garden of a book. As for the "how," that's another matter entirely. As Jesus' parable regarding the automatic earth puts it, "we know not how." I would just as soon call it the grace of God and call it a day. And therefore I will.

Introduction

*A*braham Heschel was once asked what he felt was most lacking in the modern scene. He answered with a single word: "Creatureliness." I have, over the years, continued to be intrigued by Rabbi Heschel's answer. His word, it seems, has roots in the earth, beholdenness to an otherly Creator, and a level sense about its place in between. As with any young word, "creatureliness" awaits the occasion when older words can gather around to help clarify its meaning, grown elephants circling the baby as it learns to step its way across the savanna. In my own mind, one of those words is *enough*.

By *enough* I do not mean the heel of a shoe pounded on the podium, as in "I've had it! That's enough!" Though there is much truth in William Blake's words about the tigers of wrath being wiser than the horses of instruction, I am not fit for rage, nor do any of us tend to respond so well to it. Instead, with a little help from the Wisdom tradition within Christianity, I use the idea of *enough* in a different tone of voice. I mean by it a certain disposition of adequacy grounded in an even deeper sense of abundance. The creaturely person seems to need little and offer much, owing to a balanced awareness of being neither any more nor any less than a creature of God's creating: merely a creature, and yet every bit *God's* creature.

I have taken up the idea of longing for enough in a culture of more for three reasons. The first is to acknowledge and challenge the patterns of acquisition and excess native to our kind but particularly to our culture. By "our culture" I am referring, of course, to the small fraction of the world's population inordinately possessed of goods and services both basic and extravagant. Most of the world does not wrestle with the dilemma of excessive acquisition, if only because most of the world does not have the luxury to do so. For those of us who do face this dilemma, who live in societies in which material, emotional, experiential, and even spiritual self-indulgence threatens to crowd any notions of adequacy out of the room, we must find the ways and means by which to reclaim our birthright as creatures. We must learn what it means to listen to inner longings other than the appetite for more, longings that quietly assert that enough is enough, and then to heed these sacred stirrings by the different ways we begin to live and trust.

I do not see this book's endeavor as moral high-grounding in any sense—heaven knows I swim in the same waters as most readers—but as a way of probing some alternative possibilities for how together we might practice faith and life. As Eudora Welty once put it, the idea here is not to point a finger but to part a curtain. The simple fact is that both our personal and public lives are better suited to sufficiency than saturation; that is to say, as a species we travel better light than heavy-laden. We and the weighed-down world have much to gain by reclaiming this truth and being reclaimed by it. We have much to lose by not.

Second, living with enough has to do with the company I keep. Over the course my forty-seven years, half of these as a pastor, I have known many whose lives I would consider well-lived—you've surely known them too. My friend Bill Bryan often calls them "durable saints." In most every instance, among the varied ways faithfulness has become the fabric of their lives, one quality has been identifiable again and again: Heschel's creatureliness—a certain adequacy of means that issues forth in abundance for others.

At their passing, these durable saints have signed the air not so much with fanfare as grace. The ledgers of their lives are long in matters of generosity, self-giving, and trust; more measured in the realm of acquisition and possessions; and slimmest of all in regard to recognition and self-promotion. In other words, over a lifetime they seem, to return to words from above, to have needed little and offered much.

If you were to ask them as they drew near dying day what their lives had amounted to—and many times I have—they would speak, predictably, *with* modesty but never *about* their own modest lifestyles. It is as though they were once told a divine secret whose words they soon after forgot, but whose truth they continued nonetheless to live by for the remainder of their lives. I find myself wondering what that secret is, and whether it would be possible for us to have it whispered in our ears also, then remembered just long enough to practice until learned by heart. Like these, I would like to leave this world having asked less of it than I have given to it, without having much said about the matter either way.

Finally, I turn to the question of living contentedly with enough because, in reflecting on that quality in others, I am led to wonder if this characteristic reveals a glimpse of the divine nature. If we are made in God's image, and if living by such contented sufficiency becomes us, then is there a modest aspect to God's nature? Our earlier description of those who "need little and offer much" could certainly be applied to God with no risk of overstatement. I am stirred by the notion that the God of biblical faith may be a modest God, and I wish at least to begin to explore that idea in these pages, along with its possible implications for our lives.

I have arranged the five sections of this book with the help of a single adjective, "good," a word that is often passed over in favor of the showier and more superlative "great." The way I see it, if we can still call the life-giving message that resides at the heart of our faith "good" news, if the gold standard for blessing a marriage is still "be *good* to one another," if "God is *good*" gets the last word about God in our children's mealtime prayer, then the word is fully adequate to serve, if not a great purpose, then certainly a good one. Besides, the dictionary says the root meaning of *great* is merely "large," whereas the word *good* derives from "what one clings to." Given the choice, which would you rather have over for supper? In that regard, I want to believe less can be more, not only in the pages of a book, but in the chapters of a life as well, and even in the volumes of once and future history.

These are my questions and yearnings. Perhaps they are yours too. If so, then I hope this exploration of a more "creaturely" way of life will speak to a longing in your own heart, a longing for enough to be plenty, and for a simpler life to be experienced as abundant beyond measure. From there, we just might begin to find our way to practicing such a life, such a way of being, until over time, by the benefit of grace, we come to a place where that divine secret is all but forgotten, and all that's left is a life well lived.

Describing those Christians who are willing to explore new ways of living faithfully and well, Bill Bryan uses a companion term for "durable saints." He calls them "daring saints." Daring saints work to set aside prevailing assumptions about how life is supposed to be lived and set out on a trust walk with others of discovery and discernment. Durable saints and daring saints. I suppose as much as anything else, I am inviting you in these pages to join me in becoming one. Which one? Come and see.

part
one

The Good Book

The Bible is alive, it speaks to me;
it has feet, it runs after me; it has
hands, it lays hold of me.

Martin Luther

Chapter 1

The Modesty of God

And God saw that it was good.
Genesis 1:10b

Don't you find it curious that in the entire creation account in the book of Genesis there's not a single exclamation point? No "Heavens to Betsy!" No "Have a look at this!" Not even a "Glory be!" It goes without saying that the creation account is a story of epic size and scope, drama and dimension, in which light is wrested from darkness, the sun and moon hurled into their everlasting orbits, living things brought forth from earth and sea at the very mention of their names, the great waters shoved back from the land and held spellbound, and, of course, the human creature drafted and crafted from God's very image, mere mud being the medium. Yet in all of this astonishing activity not a syllable of superlative language makes it onto the page.

The closest these accounts in Genesis come to exclamatory speech is—are you ready?—"And God saw that it was good." That's it. Once, in what we can only imagine was a flourish of unchecked enthusiasm, the narrative gives us slightly more: God saw everything that God had made, "and indeed, it was *very* good" (Genesis 1:31, even the emphasis is mine). We're talking about the making of the universe here, the very origination of who we and the world are, the biggest event history has ever been privy to, and the best God can do is "good" and "very good"? This we could call understatement of divine proportions.

I'm sure you can think of a moment in the creation event you believe might have called for at least a little hoopla, a place where the powers that be might have placed an exclamation point or two—a "totally awesome!" or an "utterly amazing!"—without being accused of getting carried away. What would be your choice? Making the light? Suspending the sun? Fashioning the human creature? Any of these could easily qualify as marquee material. What we get instead is plain print on pastel parchment, posted not under the lights but on the shelf, all matter and no mirth.

Maybe the scribe was low on ink, rationing it for essentials, or reserving exclamatory speech for the possibility of something *really* big happening later. Perhaps the story had been handled so many countless times, generation to generation, that by the time it was finally put to print it had lost some of its original language of luster and pizzazz, the way the marble feet of a statuary saint are worn away by countless years of kisses.

Or maybe there's something else involved. The creation story might be told in such dramatically undramatic speech partly as a means of showing the reader a way of viewing not only the world and ourselves within it—two things we'll have time to talk about later—but something more: a way of thinking about God, and about the way God thinks.

In these earliest verses of the Bible is a God who is portrayed not as super-Herculean, just suitably capable; not as hyper-heroic, but creative; not as melodramatic, but merely attentive. God is not lionized, but simply recognized, accounted for, presented right in with everything else, all without a great deal of flourish. Furthermore, the creating this God does is conceived not by flashing wand or rolling chariot, magic incantation or angelic host; creation is conceived by something far more pedestrian: mere words—the same garden-variety tools available to every babbling child and raving lunatic, every highway billboard and cable infomercial, every starving poet and dime-store novelist.

What I'm suggesting is this: the way we are given the creation account is modest—it is modestly executed (with few words), modestly appraised (with fewer words), and modestly recalled (with a few more words). It's the plainspoken recounting of a good day's work, six times over. What it seems to reveal, among other things, and perhaps more than any other thing, is a certain modesty on the part of God, who is seen here employing mere language to make something out of nothing, without benefit—or more to the point, without need—of either fawning audience or flexing ego, fanfare introductions as it all begins or flaunting accolades when it's all wrapped up. In the tradition of a good utility player, God just gets in there, rolls up the old sleeves, and does the job. Furthermore, once all is said and done, God takes a breather. Now I ask you—did Hercules ever take a breather? This is a modest God if we've ever seen one.

For whatever assortment of reasons, we clamor at times for God to be great, awesome, supreme, omniscient, omnipotent, and a host of other superlative things besides. We can describe this as the need for what Peter Berger once called a "sacred canopy," a way of understanding God that feels safe, strong, and unshakably sturdy. We know, of course, that God can, in some form or fashion, express many superlative attributes— God is often described as great (Psalm 145), mighty (Psalm 50), wonderful and magnificent (Isaiah 28:29), and powerful (Revelation 11:17). But as seems also to be true with people, the God we come to relate to the most transparently and trust the most deeply is not the God whose name we are likely to see in the marquee lights by virtue of being fabulous, stupendous, spectacular, incredible, or totally awesome, but the God who is simply—to borrow a word from the early pages of the Good

Book—good. Safe, strong, and sturdy is the sacred canopy spread over us by ordinary trustworthiness and love.

Where does that leave us? Perhaps with a slightly different perspective not only on God but also on those said to have been created in God's image, namely, *us*. If there is a sense in which God can be understood as modest rather than grandiose in character, then our own self-understanding may bear similar reflection. In the chapter just ahead, we'll explore that idea in greater depth. Once again, the trusty book of Genesis will be on hand to help us with that enterprise, painting a picture of a place that includes some surprisingly modest features and yet, curiously, still goes by the name of "paradise."

Chapter 2

Paradise in the Balance

I've got two tickets to paradise. Won't you pack your bags—we'll leave tonight.
Eddie Money

*W*hen you hear the word *paradise*, what comes to mind? Don't we usually think of our ideal vacation—or something like it—palm trees, soft breeze, wine and cheese, endless ease? There may be a chaise lounge in the picture, white sands, perhaps an occasional dip in the crystal-clear waters of the gentle surf, the requisite spa experience, and, of course, an abundance of delectable cuisine. Our favorite people are all there—and in the best of humor. Days and nights are filled with laughter, leisure, and relaxation. Everything is picture-perfect. Ah, paradise!

You'll think I'm crazy, but I've got a question: Is there work in your picture of paradise? Let me rush to my own defense: the question wasn't my idea. Paradise is where you *don't* work—that's the whole point, right? If we think of paradise as a glorified vacation, well, what is a vacation but getting away—emphasis on the word *away*—from work? Any mention of the w-word in the context of the paradise described above is likely to get a person scowled right off the beach.

As soon as you're done scowling, listen to this: the garden of

Eden, the place from which we draw our images of the original "paradise," is more about work than pleasure. That's right—there's a time clock in paradise and punch cards. In both creation stories (Genesis 1:28-31; 2:15-22), we are given the idea right from the get-go that work is central to the human creature's idyllic existence. I'm not talking about the "punishment phase" after that little mishap with the serpent. I mean before that, when, as Browning put it, God was in heaven, and all was right with the world. Words about work are sewn into these earliest narratives like buttons on a jacket: "God blessed them, and God said to them, 'Be fruitful and multiply, and fill the earth and subdue it; and have dominion . . .'" (Genesis 1:28). "The LORD God took the man and put him in the garden of Eden to till it and keep it" (Genesis 2:15).

That second "paradise" picture almost gives us the idea that we were created *with a job in mind!* Just earlier in this narrative, before our kind ever appeared on the scene, the humans' advent is anticipated as those who will eventually be on hand "to till the ground" (2:5). Imagine the divine logic: "Hmmm, all these nice things I've created—fruit trees, lovely grasses, flowers, shrubs. They're definitely going to need some looking after—watering, weeding, pruning. I think I'll fashion a creature who can take care of this place. Let's see, something with an eye for beauty and a strong back."

Some paradise! Till and tend; be fruitful and multiply. Work a lot; play a little. That sounds more like *real life* than paradise! And yet that pattern, or rhythm, is precisely what we find in the first paradise called the garden of Eden: a balance between labor and leisure, effort and ease. What that picture seems to tell us, among other things, is that, to borrow a popular idiom, *it's not all about us.* We were created not to be indulged and pampered as though we were baby royalty who were plopped down one day into the very lap of the universe, complete with instructions for our care and feeding. Instead, the care and feeding instructions come to *us*, to wit: Make yourselves useful;

13

oh, yes, and while you're at it, you're free to enjoy both the fruits of your labors and those of the naturally occurring variety. So have at it—get your hands dirty *and* glory in the good earth that gets them so.

Didn't God also have *us* in mind in the creating task? I know the psalms say we are the *apple* of God's eye, but surely creation wasn't all about fruits and vegetables with us as an add-on. Of course it wasn't—we're a unique part of the labyrinth of the created order. It's just that all by ourselves we would make a fairly unimpressive cornucopia. As Madeleine L'Engle puts it in *Glimpses of Grace*, we are "portion, not pinnacle" of creation. To begin with, we weren't the first thing out of the chute. Things were beautiful and good even before we existed. Secondly, once we showed up, there were limbs to be pruned, and seeing as how the tree frogs didn't come with opposable digits, that left ours truly to operate the lopping shears. If we are *cherished* by God, we are also *charged* by God. We may be the apple of God's eye, but the other fruit varieties still need tending.

Genesis, then, gives us a rather different picture of paradise than the one we tend to carry around in our mind's eye. If the Good Book is our guide, then the good life is a life in which we are not only provid*ed* for but also provid*ing* for—and not necessarily in that order. Paradise appears to be found in the balancing of work and pleasure, others and self, obligation and leisure, belonging and freedom; which is where the notion of modesty comes in. One of the meanings of the word *modesty* is "middle." Modesty is a characteristic, or way of life, which would situate us in the middle, between extremes of all work or all leisure. This is just where the first human pair found themselves: not enslaved but not pampered, not neglected but not mollycoddled, not underfed but neither spoon-fed, working and resting, tending to other facets of creation yet also feeding themselves, neither heroic nor hedonistic—artfully balanced between the two.

In that artful balance, the story of the first paradise tilts slightly in favor of output over input, rather like the durable saints I mentioned in the introduction—needing little, offering much. There's a line perhaps some of our grandparents used to dish out if we were ever lazing around getting in the way of someone else's work: "Make yourself useful," they would say. It's close to what happens here in Genesis, only with God doing the making and us doing the useful.

We have other options, of course, such as pretending all of this isn't so—that for us, at least, paradise is all about bonbons. We'll see directly just how quickly a cottage industry grew up around that particular fiction. For the time being, however, we should at least agree that the picture of paradise painted in the earliest pages in the Bible is one which foresees at least as many blisters as bonbons.

We'll have a look next at how things turned south—actually, east—from that original modest paradisal arrangement. For that purpose, we turn briefly to the second narrative in Genesis, a story involving a serpent, a man, a woman, and a certain tree known for its low-lying fruit.

Chapter 3

What We Need Is Here

In America it is difficult to achieve a sense of enough.
John Updike

I claim to be no expert on the little dalliance recorded in Genesis 3 between two humans and the snake. From what I understand, the episode has to do with good and evil, limits and liabilities, greed, naiveté, and some serious myopia, all more or less played out in a couple of sidewinding conversations. On this one Genesis story countless books have been written, scores of sermons preached, and infinite lectures given, including, in the latter case, of the homespun variety, just before the car keys are handed over or just after they're taken away. As with all the good stories in Scripture, this one reads us like a book, and since it is always more difficult to make sense of ourselves than of somebody else, we tend to hem and haw as to its precise meaning for our lives.

What seems clear enough is that, in something of a dismissal of the proverb, *a bird in the hand is worth two in the bush,* Eve and Adam were enticed to the tree in question in part because it promised something more than what they had. And who could blame them for thinking of paradise the same way you and I tend to do; that is, if a little pleasure is good, then more is surely better. Watch this tantalizing logic rise like pastry in the oven: "So when the woman saw that the tree was *good for food,* and that is was a *delight to the eyes,* and that the tree was to be *desired* to make one wise . . ." (Genesis 3:6, emphasis added). With its alluringly luscious language advancing a rather attractive fiction as to how life might be lived, there's one thing we can say for sure: When this series of unfortunate events unfolded, Eve definitely had all her senses about her. Pure pleasure had come to call.

What Eve and Adam soon learn is one of the plainest and yet most elusive of all of life's truths: pure pleasure never is. If we don't learn this axiom from our scholarly studies of Mrs. Piggle-Wiggle and the girl who would eat nothing but chocolate, or from the early pages of Genesis, we learn it from that other unfailing source of instruction—life itself. Experience teaches us that genuine pleasure always comes in packages in which other items appear higher in the list of ingredients— items such as work, effort, responsibility, reasonableness, self-forgetfulness, and attentiveness to others. As with curry powder or habanero sauce, a small amount of pleasure goes a long way.

Just as true and doubly odd is that inordinate attempts at pleasure usually leave us bereft rather than blissful. Much of what the serpent promised the pair was already theirs, until they reached for more, at which point it all evaporated, and they were left chafing in their fig leaves. Listen for the familiar: "God knows that when you eat of [the tree that is in the middle of the garden] your eyes will be opened, and you will be like God, knowing good and evil." Let's take these enticements one at a time. "Eyes opened"? Maybe the serpent was employing poetic license here, but we know the pair can at least see the serpent, and we've already been told that the tree under discussion was a "delight to the eyes." "Like God"? It's already been chronicled that the two were made in God's spitting image— the creation story says so *four times over* (1:26-27)! "Knowing good and evil"? This one's a little tricky because getting our minds around the meaning of the phrase "good and evil" is about like a dog trying to bite a basketball. In the sense that the words mean right and wrong, these two are definitely there before the big bite. Eve has already explained right from wrong to the serpent earlier in the conversation: "We may eat" of all these trees. That would be *right*. "You shall not eat" of one particular tree. This fits into the category known to professional ethicists and little mischief-makers alike as *wrong*.

To be sure, when the pair went ahead with the taste test their eyes *were* opened, in a manner of speaking, and a certain sense of good and evil was attained. We might even say they became more like God, in the sense of learning what it means to ache for a world that has squandered its original freedom. In any event, their "acquisitions" were nothing to write home about, for in a single instant the pleasure was all mined. The peak, as it turns out, was in the imagining, not the satisfying, of their interest. Keats said it well: "Heard melodies are sweet, but those unheard are sweeter."

To choose to be content with such a paradise as Adam and Eve were enjoying before the serpent appeared on the scene would seem a no-brainer. Instead, the two made a choice that could only be described as a different sort of no-brainer, as in "What were they thinking?" The pair and their story remind us that reaching for more of what we already possess in suitable abundance tends to leave us with the short end of the stick. From our childhood we've heard the story of a dog with a bone. It sees reflected in a pond what appears to be a dog with a slightly bigger bone. The dog determines to go after the bone it sees reflected in the water and winds up with a lost bone and a blurry reflection. What looks from the outset like a great deal—in Adam and Eve's case, yummy, delightful, and enlightening—turns out to be what in Spanish we sometimes call a *carcachita*, which roughly translated means "a bucket of bolts masquerading as a car."

Adam and Eve's story reminds us of a fundamental reality regarding the moral life. Choosing well is about more than knowing what is right, even though that information is surely important. Something else is called for in making good choices. Is it self-reflection? Is it taking perspective? Perhaps it is the slowly dawning awareness, usually learned over years or even an entire lifetime, that the prospect of "more," though awakening appetites that run fairly deep within us, is not ultimately satisfying. "Enough," while rather more lacking in curb appeal, has proven over countless generations to be a trustworthy tool for gauging what we really need.

In the closing words of a Sabbath poem, "The Wild Geese," Wendell Berry reflects that our truest yearning is not to grasp at things that are out there somewhere

> *. . . but to be*
> *quiet in heart, and in eye*
> *clear. What we need is here.*

He seems to be saying that the life to which we most deeply aspire is not somewhere up in the trees, but down on the earth. What we need is not more, but an awareness of what we already possess and are possessed by. What we need is not always elsewhere and otherwise, coming soon, just over that next horizon, right after that next deal, next job, next purchase, next promotion. What we need has already been looked after. *What we need is here.*

Chapter 4

The Future of an Illusion

We teach our children one thing only,
as we were taught: to wake up.
Annie Dillard

*W*hat were some of your illusions as a child? I remember thinking my wonderful third grade student teacher, Miss Rose, surely loved her class of children more than whatever other things her future might hold, such as graduation, gainful employment, or marriage and family, and therefore she would never leave us. One day the unthinkable happened: our teacher announced that Miss Rose had completed her appointed time with us and would be saying goodbye the following week. I was crestfallen. Though I recovered nicely, I had learned—at some level anyway—a valuable lesson: the world was bigger than my classroom, and certainly than my heart.

Illusions don't leave us at childhood's end, of course. Many of them evaporate, but they are often replaced by others. As a result, years later, grown up as we might be in so many ways, we continue to harbor illusions of all sorts. The garden of our lives may be filled with many fruitful trees, but the serpent lurks among them, cultivating a particular deceit just suited to our cravings. We've already looked at a handful of these illusions: "Life is about figuring out how to work less and relax more"; "More is always better"; "It's all about me"; and "Fruit within reach is ours for the taking."

Another stalwart illusion, practically foundational in cultural lore, is that of the "self-made man" or woman—the idea that, in a technique defying various laws of physics, it is possible to pull ourselves up by our own bootstraps, and in such a way to succeed in life entirely independent of any help from anyone else. We even have a saying for it, often advanced with biblical conviction: "God helps those who help themselves." The fact that the phrase is not found in the Bible seems to be of little importance to those who hold the view. It functions quite well to reinforce the illusion of self-generated success. I remember a poster that satirizes this particular illusion beautifully: a boy of twelve or so, sporting casual clothes and designer sunglasses, leans back against a very expensive sports car, a look of cool satisfaction on his face. Beneath, the caption reads, "I've worked hard all my life for this."

If illusions can be seemingly beneficial to those harboring them, they can also lead to many destructive—not to mention unbecoming—behaviors for everyone involved. The illusion of self-generated success, for instance, often carries with it certain attitudes of detachment. If I have made my own way through life, then my need for and accountability to God and others is dismissible. Furthermore, if I don't need God or others, then neither do God or others have any claim on me.

Enter the prophets of the Bible, a group whose charge it was from God to awaken people of faith from their illusions and replace these with reality. "Speaking truth to power" is the way the Quakers have traditionally described the prophetic role, a reference to the dynamic often at work between prophet and audience. The prophet is given a word from God that essentially states the obvious, that is, the truth: "You behave as though you created yourself and are beholden to no one. In point of fact, God is your Creator, and you draw your very sustenance from the God-given community that surrounds you, reared you, and will one day lay you to rest in the good earth. It is time you honor those sources of life, treat them fairly, love them faithfully, return their kindness. You may be nicely fixed up at the moment, but your primrose path is verging on a slippery slope."

That would be the "truth" part. The "power" part is that these words were generally spoken to people who couldn't be bothered and who possessed the ability to squash you like a bug for daring to say such inconvenient things. This could be a sovereign, a group of temple priests, or even the common people, in which case, many hands can make light work of a meddlesome prophet. "The word of the Lord *came to* so-and-so" is a phrase you see often in the introductory lines of a prophetic book. "So-and-so *came to* the word of the Lord," on the other hand, is a phrase you won't see much of. When we look at some of the occupational hazards of the role, we can understand why being a prophet is not for the interested; it is only for the conscripted.

Drawing upon the Quaker definition, I'd like to word the dynamic in a slightly different way: prophesy as speaking truth to *illusion*. After all, prophets more often than not simply said what was true, the problem being the limited inclination of the hearer to appropriate true information. As T. S. Eliot once put it, "Humankind cannot bear very much reality." What the prophets did again and again was speak about reality in settings where reality had long since been reasoned away to make room for illusions. To entire communities that had come to be structured around false ways of living and relating, the prophets lifted their voices, and spoke the truth.

If we could summarize the overall plea of these divinely driven prophets and their relentless efforts to wake those asleep at the wheel, it might be best done with the paraphrased words of Micah, a minor prophet with a major message: "[God] has told you, O mortal, what is good; and what does the Lord require of you but to do justice, and to love kindness, and to walk humbly with your God?" (Micah 6:8)

As we can see from Micah's message, what the prophets asked for from their hearers was not the world, but something far more reasonable: for their lives to be lived decently in both horizontal and vertical dimensions, fair and responsible relationships within the community, coupled with a relationship with God of sensible regard. The divine will these prophets brought to expression in their exhortations was not for ultimate destruction and condemnation, but healing and reconciliation. Their harsh and heavy words were intended not for harm but for good. When it comes to God's message as conveyed through the prophets, judgment is really mercy in disguise.

A pastoral counselor I visited several times during seminary had a poster in his office depicting a rag doll being squeezed through the rollers of a ringer washer. Underneath, the caption read, "The truth will make you free . . . but first it will make you miserable." Let's see now. To be made free? Sure, I'll take free—no argument there. Miserable, then free? Hmmm, I'll have to give that one some thought.

As far as the prophets are concerned, the only way to freedom for the individual or the community is to shed the illusions that, while we find them so very convenient, leave us—and the world—severely wanting. The prophets' call to us is to begin living with eyes and hearts open to an unrelenting and unapologetic reality, to wit: The immodesty with which we "self-made" ones are prone to make our merry little way through life calls for too wide a swath on too narrow a path to be morally or practically reasonable. God and others need us to share the road, and, in a curious way, we need them to need us to do so. God is to be honored, as are the poor and vulnerable. The earth is to be tended with care, and our lives are to be awakened to their original blessing of *enough*. It is all a matter of whittling us not so much down to size as *up* to size. God knows we are made for a better way. If we do not find this way, this way will find us, courtesy of those who did not come to the word of the Lord, but to whom the word of the Lord did come.

Chapter 5

Weaning the Soul

*There is enormous value in Eastern and Western spiritual
disciplines, but they guarantee nothing. Their value is
greatest when they help us lighten our greedy, self-serious
striving—when they free us to be self-forgetfully, gently,
simply present, here and now . . .*
Tilden Edwards

The prophets call us to shed our illusions, but how? They tell
us to look at the world in a different way, but by what
means? They announce to us God's intention that we do justice,
love mercy, and walk modestly with God, but where is the compass for that walk? If I am to be more aware of the world around
me, I will certainly need to be more self-aware, but *not*, for
heaven's sake, more self-absorbed. How do I find this balance
between self-attention for the purpose of honest examination and
self-forgetfulness for the purpose of loving and serving others?

When you need something, whether it's a cup of flour or an
honest answer, a close neighbor is always a good place to turn.
In the case of the prophetic works, one close neighbor is the
book of Psalms, a good source for both flour and honesty. The
Psalms comprise the Bible's largest book, and hidden within
them is one of the Bible's tiniest prayers, Psalm 131. This psalm

is of such a size and character that it could easily be overlooked for an entire lifetime, even by a student of the Bible. By the same token, it has such a demeanor about it, such an outlook on life, such an intriguing way of regarding God and the soul, that once it gains more than passing notice, it is not easily forgotten. Is this because the psalm offers a prayer, but never asks for anything? Perhaps it is because the psalm speaks in that rarest of modern volumes: just above a whisper. Maybe the psalm remains with the imagination, and in the heart, because at its center is one of the tenderest images in all of Scripture—one could even say in all of life: a mother and her young child. For whatever assortment of reasons, Psalm 131, once discovered, is difficult to part with. See if you don't agree:

> O LORD, my heart is not lifted up,
>   my eyes are not raised too high;
> I do not occupy myself with things
>   too great and too marvelous for me.
> But I have calmed and quieted my soul,
>   like a weaned child with its mother;
>   my soul is like the weaned child that is with me.
> O Israel, hope in the LORD
>   from this time on and forevermore.

In the presence of such a prayer as this, one doesn't quite know whether to slip quietly from the room out of respect or simply to hush the breathing and listen in. For whatever reason, we are granted the privilege of the latter—to stay and overhear the deeply earnest self-revealing of another human being before God. There is something—what is the word?—*silencing* about such a shared experience. A whispered prayer, for one who happens to overhear it, is a hushing experience indeed.

This psalm is the closest we may ever come to identifying a biblical text as having been set down by a woman's hand. The parallels are entirely suggestive of this possibility: my soul is to me as a child is to its mother, as *the child that is with me* is to me. The psalmist appears to be drawing upon the personal identity of young motherhood to cast a metaphor regarding the soul. For our purposes, then, we will refer to the psalmist from here forward as a woman.

Taken together, verses one and two of Psalm 131 reveal a loom at work, weaving together surrender and self-possession. First, the surrender: the person who prays this prayer seems to have arrived at a place of having patiently and purposefully yielded up life's grand pursuits—or to borrow from our discussion just earlier, life's grand illusions, all as a process of weaning the soul to autonomy and self-surrender. As a result of such choices and practices, the present moment situates her in a place that is, from every indication, a place of true self-awareness, contentment, quiet, and calm.

How does she achieve such contentment? The first verse is clearly a portal, a doorway to that peaceable life: the decision to deliberately relinquish the preoccupation with better/more/greater/higher. E. Stanley Jones summarized the Christian life in that one word: surrender. To give up our feeble efforts to live by tired and time-spent illusions is the first movement toward that place of utter adequacy in which the psalmist finds herself. Contentment begins with redirection of our attention away from things beyond both reach and reason.

However, identifying what we've chosen to avoid or surrender does little in and of itself to satisfy the longing heart. If nothing replaces these lost means of support, we are like the house in Jesus' story—one evil spirit leaves, only to return with seven others (Matthew 12:43-45). The second part of this mother's prayer turns our focus inward, toward the cultivation of what Fulton J. Sheen called "invisible means of support": *But I have calmed and quieted my soul.*

"Calm" and "quiet" are, in the Hebrew, verbs of intensive action, applied in a manner of deliberate tending. From this we might gather that spiritual contentedness comes through a sort of hyper-vigilant responsiveness to the soul's every need, as though my soul were meant to be the centerpiece of my time and attention. This idea would certainly strike a chord, for if widespread spiritual neglect has an equal in our society, it may be widespread spiritual indulgence—the notion that the way we should attend to our spiritual lives is the way we would care for an expensive sports car or exotic pet—with a great deal of preening and pampering. It is an attractive notion, with a good many adherents within the Christian subculture, as it conveniently reflects a broader assumption regarding self-care—one of the illusions mentioned earlier: if a little is good, then more must be better.

Interestingly, the presenting metaphor in the psalm offers a more nuanced picture of what care of the soul looks like. If the soul is analogous to a weaned child, then the operative means of care is not pampering but *withdrawal*. A weaned child is a child whose dependency has been deliberately and systematically moderated over time in a gradual, nurturing process of moving from breast to bottle, bottle to cup, cup to kitchen and fending for yourself. The soul in question is not a coddled soul, doted over to the satisfaction of its every whim. This soul has come of age, its nursing appetite gently redirected in the interest of greater autonomy. By the mother's initiative, the cutting of the apron strings has begun.

We know from experience that the best support we can offer others—or others, us—in family or friendship, supervision or spiritual nurture, manages a middle path between molly-coddling and neglect. So it is with the work of caring for our interior lives. Our souls do not require five-star service; they need garden-variety cultivation. As in Eden, so in our spiritual lives, there is such a thing as too much—too much attention, too much accommodation, too much "care." Digging up the seedling each day to check on its progress may give the appearance of deep concern, but as any preschooler will tell you, the outcome leaves a muddier picture.

Spiritual maturity, it would seem, is a matter of attending and ignoring, each in the right measure. "Teach us to care and not to care," wrote T. S. Eliot. His words could be describing the sense of modest balance that allows the care of the soul to proceed not excessively, but moderately. The phrase is lifted from a poem entitled "Ash Wednesday," a reference to the threshold of the forty-day season of Lent, during which we practice together caring more and caring less—more about God's redeeming work through Christ in the world, less about all besides.

Lest our lives become enveloped in ambitions and pursuits of which the prophets warn, this simple prayer's beginning words draw us nearer the disposition of surrender. Lest our lives become enveloped in the construction of our own inner hideaway to the neglect of the wayfaring world for which the prophets weep, the prayer's maternal tone weans us from spiritual self-indulgence. Tending the soul is deliberate but evenly wrought, the goal being self-forgetfulness for the sake of others.

O Israel, hope in the LORD *from this time on and forevermore.* The psalmist now pulls away from her lingering prayer as a mother generates distance from her weaning child, and in keeping with the pledge she has made to God, turns her attention to the needs that widen beyond her door. Hers now is the work of bringing hope to that wayfaring world. Her diminutive presence, slight as a whisper, now swells in measured confidence to ask of the world a certain height and, in the same breath, to offer it a certain assurance: *Hope in the Lord forever.* Her mode of prayer and loving comes very near the pattern of Thomas Merton: "I disappear from the world as an object of interest in order to be everywhere by hiddenness and compassion." The soul, having now receded from the spotlight, is ready to love.

Chapter 6

Risking Reverence

The first condition of human goodness is something to love; the second, something to reverence.
George Eliot

So far we've been looking at the Old Testament, or Hebrew Scripture, for insight into what it means to live with a sense of adequacy before God. Rounding the cape, we now make our way to the gospels and their central figure, Jesus, to consider the same question. What did Jesus teach his followers about having enough? And what do these teachings suggest for the way we live our own lives?

One way to answer that question is to look at a prayer Jesus taught his disciples to pray. It is, in and of itself, a modest prayer, only a few lines in length, and taking less than a minute to pray. For size, it certainly doesn't dominate the landscape of the Gospels. As for style, it's relatively plain. For what it holds within it, however, it makes a world.

> Father, hallowed be your name.
>   Your kingdom come.
>   Give us each day our daily bread.
>   And forgive us our sins,
>   for we ourselves forgive everyone indebted to us.
>   And do not bring us to the time of trial. (Luke 11:2-4)

The world this prayer makes is mostly familiar, even pedestrian, made up as it is of various household words—Father, bread, forgiveness, trials. Even "your kingdom come" is recognizable as a petition for God's good and just purposes to be fully realized in our world. But there is one word in the prayer that most of us would agree is a little curious, a word we could probably go for whole days without using in a conversation: *hallowed*.

What does *hallowed* mean? Knowing that would probably be your next question, I looked it up ahead of time. *Hallowed* means "holy," or "set apart." Halloween, for example, or "All Hallows' Eve," refers to the night before All Hallows' or All Saints' Day, when we celebrate the "holy ones," that is, those *set apart* in baptism as belonging to God. The Indo-European roots of the word are also instructive, suggesting meanings of "whole" and "uninjured."

The grammatical form of the phrase we're looking at in the Lord's Prayer is what we call—if we're ever in a situation where we need to call it anything at all—an implied modal auxiliary verb form, which simply means the main verb sequence, in this case, "be hallowed," is supported by an assumed secondary verb of hope or desire, as in "*May* your name be hallowed." All of this said, the meaning of Jesus' words begins to come clear: Father, may your name be revered, regarded as holy, held as sacred. May the world's conception of who you are be whole and uninjured.

This is the first thing Jesus says in the prayer he teaches his disciples to pray. Before a single petition is voiced, a single pledge given, a single acclamation offered, he expresses a fundamental longing, a yearning for God's name to be revered, held sacred. Imagine you were crafting a once-and-for-all prayer for your congregation to pray; what would you put first? Praise, perhaps? Confession? Thanksgiving? A petition of some sort? Would it even occur to you to start this universal prayer with an expression of longing for holiness?

Perhaps you might begin your prayer this way if deep within you had a yearning for God to be known by the children of your congregation, and the youth, as well as the adults, as kind and loving, strong but gentle, wise and knowing. Perhaps you might if deep within you ached for the world to rediscover its misplaced capacity for awe. Perhaps you might begin your prayer in such a way if you yourself felt a need deep within to honor something beyond yourself, namely your Creator, to hold in unspeakable regard the God who made you, loves you, and made those whom you love, the God who created the very world in which you live and move and have your being. Only if we had to name some reality in whose presence we would be hard pressed not to weep in wonder—only then would we teach a prayer that began in the way Jesus' prayer begins, *Hallowed be your name*.

In one of her lectures, Kathleen Norris commented that sometimes "we lose our touch, and shift from praise to appraisal." I take her to mean that, drawing near something awesome, wondrous, or inspiring, we are inclined almost immediately to begin to dismantle it, dissect it, deconstruct it, explain it away. Some combination of a marketing culture, political skepticism, spiritual cynicism, and Hollywood special effects has left our generation with a well-developed command of the phrase, "Nuh-uh."

In that context, to pray *Hallowed be your name* is the first step in healing the stiff-arming of our age, gradually lowering the drawbridge to the castle of our hearts, where we seem born to adore and only later learn not to. To pray this strange and blessed prayer is to risk a reverence that allows for a divine mystery bigger than all of us. When we lift our voices together in such an expression, then the secret is out: we belong to a community that yearns along with Jesus for the world's regard for God to be uninjured, which is to say, for a rekindling of our creaturely capacity for meeting holiness with awe.

When this occurs, it is not merely God who is hallowed; the hearts of those who practice such reverence are increasingly made "whole" and "uninjured." To risk reverence is to begin to see ourselves in the middle place to which prayer of any sort always leads us: raised up by the confidence of children who are blessed with a listening God and leveled out by the awareness that this God, who is beyond our figuring or fathoming, has been known to capitalize on the slightest opportunity to make us holy.

My friend John Thornburg has set the Matthew triumphal entry narrative into poetic verse as part of a Palm Sunday cantata. In one segment, he gives voice to the man who is approached by Jesus' disciples for a colt and its mother, imagining what his response to such a demand might have been.

> *I did not know these messengers*
> *with pool-deep feelings in their eyes.*
> *I thought that I would spend my days*
> *untouched by wonder and surprise.*
>
> *"We need your colt, its mother, too.*
> *The Lord has need of them today."*
> *I felt a shudder in my heart.*
> *I could not think. I could not pray.*
>
> *Who is this enigmatic Lord?*
> *Will they be coming next for me?*
>
> *This bold request has changed my world;*
> *Shalom has knocked upon my door.*
> *I do not know what is to come;*
> *I only know I ache for more.*

Do you find yourself going through life with the assumption that you will spend your days "untouched by wonder or surprise"? Hear this good news: completely beyond all expectations, *shalom*, which is the Bible's word for "wholeness," is on its way to knock upon your door and make a bold request—We need your colt, its mother, too . . . and *you*. In that breathless moment, when more is asked than you have to give and more given than you could possibly ask, you will cease to describe yourself as "untouched." For to open the door to God's holiness is to begin to experience the widening gift of wonder. The heart begins to rearrange itself, and that old friend, cynicism, along with other jaded attitudes, all stand a good chance of being put out on the curb. One should prepare for such outcomes, remembering that reverence entails risk.

part two

The Good Life

God in my sufficing . . .

Carmina Gadelica III

Chapter 7

Longing for Enough

*"What do you think the cow sees with her big
brown eyes?" Mary asked.
"Oh, many things," Jeremy answered, "but mostly
grass."*

Carrie Lou Goddard,
God, You Are Always with Us

*W*hat does "the good life" consist of? How do we begin in
our everyday lives to "walk modestly before God," to
put into practice the notion of "needing little and offering
much"? By now we've visited some of the stories and messages
of the Bible for insights into those questions. In this section,
we'll consider more closely what it means to live well in the
context of those insights. I'd like to start with a look at various
inner urges, and ways in which these find their appropriate
places in the life well lived.

We could say that there are generally two sorts of urges we
feel and act upon in our daily lives. For our purposes, let's call
these appetites and longings. In my mind, appetites are hand-
to-mouth sorts of urges such as eating, resting, and finding
immediate pleasure, stimulation, or satiety from various
sources. Longings tend to be, as the word suggests, "longer" in

character—they are the stuff of dreams, hopes, memories, relationships, and spiritual and vocational direction, and have more of an enduring quality. Appetites might vary from hour to hour—even minute to minute; longings tend to abide for an extended period—perhaps a lifetime. One further difference—appetites can often be satisfied in isolation, whereas longings of the sort I mean tend to involve others in their fulfillment.

We tend to think of longings as future-oriented, but they can just as easily tug at us from behind. Aches and pains are a by-product not merely of aging, but of living, and are not only physical but spiritual and emotional as well. The aches and pains of grief, resentment, guilt, missed opportunities, lost relationships—you name it (and you could)—all leave us longing for a meeting of minds, hearts, and grace. *One Hundred Years of Solitude* begins its epic tale with a haunting reminder that simply because love is lost does not mean it is forgotten: "It was inevitable: the scent of bitter almonds always reminded him of the fate of unrequited love." Love unrequited, wounded, lost, unexpressed—these are among the things we can see through the rearview mirror, in which, as they say, objects are closer than they appear.

Here's what's tricky: longings sometimes masquerade as appetites. What we think is an appetite urge is often really an unrecognized longing. Or perhaps we recognize that longing plainly, but rather than seek to fulfill it, we take a more immediate and convenient approach and fill some vague appetite instead. I recently came across a memo pad with the following caption: "When I'm trying to make a decision, I always listen to my gut. It usually tells me to eat chocolate."

Perhaps one of the most difficult lessons in life—at least in modern life—is learning the difference between a longing and an appetite. What urges are deep and enduring and can await their time, or even go forever unfulfilled, and which are immediate and urgent and call for immediate attention, or not?

Sometimes it's difficult to know. It doesn't help a great deal that we are immersed in a marketing culture born and bred to convince us that every longing that tugs at us is really an appetite making an irrepressible demand that it be satisfied *right away*. In other words, our gut is not the only thing telling us to eat chocolate—an entire society encircles us with that message, samples in hand.

There is, for each of us, a custom-made set of reasons that the longings we feel sometimes impersonate appetites, and therefore go unaddressed in any enduring sense. The work of discovering those reasons, however, can be very much like untangling a fishing line. How do we learn the difference between a longing and an appetite, and pay proper attention to each? Not swiftly, not alone, and—here's the strange part— not necessarily by pouring a lot of resources into the project. The answers to why we behave in the ways we do are elusive, and peering deep into the psyche with headlamp and tool kit does not always result in first-rate repairs. Sometimes the brighter the searchlight, the darker and deeper the nooks and crannies become.

Holding a little more lightly to the whole matter may be a more enlightening approach. The word *appetite* actually shares a root with the word *feather*, as in "light as a —." As we grow to learn the difference between different inner tugs, we may begin, by grace, to gently finesse our responses in the direction of addressing longings when they come to call instead of darting immediately toward an ersatz appetite. In the process, some of those appetites just might begin to wither away for lack of nourishment.

For now, I have another question: Appetites aside, what do you *long* for? When you feel like you're hungry but know you're really not, what are you really "hungry" for? When you think you're short on purses or power tools but have a closet full of each, what are you really short on? This sounds kind of backwards, but I often think that the more we indulge our appetites, the deeper our longings grow. It may be precisely the closet full of purses or power tools that leaves me with a vague sense of needing something else. Is it another purse? Another power tool? Another promotion? Another partner? Let's try that and see. And the longing grows deeper. The French have a saying, coined by their sixteenth-century philosopher Rabelais: *L' appetit vient en mangeant,* or "The appetite comes by eating." If the appetite comes by eating, and longings grow deeper as we ignore them by feeding our appetites instead, before long we're straddling two circus ponies that are beginning to head in different directions.

Perhaps one of the most rudimentary longings we ever feel is the longing for enough, or rather, for enough to be enough. Maybe you know that longing already; you've come to a place of experiencing, as Frederick Buechner once put it the "too-muchness and too-littleness" of your life and are wanting somehow to live with a greater sense of sufficiency. Henry David Thoreau, who spent a couple of years eking out an existence next to Walden Pond, just west of Boston, wrote that we are rich in proportion to the number of things that we can afford to let alone. I tend to think that the urges that lead us to acquire more and more and more—purses, power tools, promotions (oh, yes—and chocolate)—are at least partly urges for the very *opposite*, longings to *shed* some of these accretions and walk on through life less encumbered and more attentive, less self-absorbed, and more aware of the world around us, richer, finally, for what we have chosen to let alone.

A seeker named Augustine, living in the fourth century, knew all about appetites as well as longings. An intellectual with a robust inclination to promiscuity, he lived large in terms of satisfying appetites both physical and philosophical. His long, meandering story of emerging from that life into one more faithful and fulfilling is told in his autobiography, *The*

Confessions. In that book appears a prayer that has become a prayer for the ages: *Everlasting God, in whom we live and move and have our being: You have made us for Yourself, so that our hearts are restless until they rest in You.*

When we're longing for this, that, and the other, chances are what we are really longing for is a sense of enough. And when we are longing for enough, odds are what we are really longing for is the One who longs for us as well, longs to be our sufficiency from cradle to grave. This is the One who alone can help us lighten our appetites, order our longings, and bring our restless hearts the one thing for which they are practically engineered to yearn: rest in God.

Chapter 8

Temples Well-aging

*Do you not know that your body is a
temple of the Holy Spirit?*
1 Corinthians 6:19

*W*hat is the body for? What claims does it make on us,
and how should we respond? How are body and mind
related? Body and spirit? We are surely more than our bodies,
but in what sense? Likewise, our bodies are more than we, but
how so? If we were to dive into these heady philosophical questions here and now, I have a gut feeling the exercise would
swallow us up, body and soul. And mind. And heart. And spirit.
And . . . you get the picture.

Perhaps there is a simpler set of questions we can try on for
size: How are we to regard these wonderfully made bodies in
which we find ourselves? And what does adequacy mean when
applied to the way we carry our physical selves through life?
Let's start by eliminating some less desirable options.

Some have regarded the body as foil, or obstacle, to the spiritual life. In this view, the body is a problem, a handicap, a
seducer or seductress, or—*yawn*—simply irrelevant. It is the
cumbersome counterpart to a nimble soul seeking its true freedom. It gets *in* the way more than it helps us *on* the way, and we
wait patiently for the day when it will get *out* of the way so our

soul can be released to God. The classical Greeks liked this idea, and so do some modern Americans. The Bible doesn't, particularly. There's too much delight with dirt in the Hebrew-Christian worldview, too much appreciation of sense and sensibility to dismiss the body as an impediment or obstacle to the sacred journey. Physicality, our tradition holds, is a great deal of trouble, but so life-giving—not to mention beautiful—that it's worth every gray hair and wrinkle.

Just a kiss away from seeing the body as foil is regarding it as a creature of comfort. Instead of employing suspicion in the relationship of self and body, the operative idea is accommodation—attending to all the wants and wishes that come our way. Listen to every whim, satisfy every appetite, follow through with every fetish. Let your body talk, then do what it says. Hungry? Eat. Thirsty? Drink. Greedy? Acquire. Angry? Curse. Lusty? Satisfy. Thereby do we come to eat too much, drink too much, spend too much, exercise too little, and with many other such socially acceptable excesses betray the body's innate need for . . . not quite so much.

If the Bible loves soil and the senses, it also has a head on its shoulders and knows that life cannot possibly be well lived simply by following the dictates of the mood ring on our pinky finger. Nor, when you think about it, is the "lap of luxury" any place for grown-ups. Laps are for babies—maybe toddlers if they push their luck; the rest of us belong in regular seating. Human creatures are called to lives that override excessive comfort and self-indulgence in favor of other commitments, such as adulthood.

Just an arm's reach from the "comfortable creature" philosophy is that which sees the body as an idol, a view that wins in every contest the admiration of the American public. In this view, the body is to be maintained with the greatest of care. I may spend two minutes a week cultivating my inner life but am respected for the hours I spend working out, cooking organically, and reading up on preventive health. Age-defying treatments follow this line of logic, with both their purpose and expense justified on the basis of understanding my body as the primary definition of who I am. As we all know in our more honest moments, aging is a reality that may be deferred briefly, but not permanently. You might take away the wrinkles, but others will eventually replace them. You can buy the little red sports car, but it will soon enough begin to show its own signs of aging—not to mention work wonders on your lower back.

Three other views of the body suggest themselves in answer to the less-than-satisfactory ideas we've looked at, views which are friendlier to our faith and, as it happens, to our close companion the body as well. These see the body as tool, teacher, and temple.

The body has infinite capacities for usefulness, an idea we'll explore more fully in the section ahead. Our bodies will sweat equally well when partying hard or when engaged in the work of perfecting a chiseled abdomen, but they look the most at home in their skin when the sweat is the result of undertakings such as sweeping the sidewalk, feeding the hungry, or worshiping God. We could say that physical exertion for a purpose beyond ourselves is an evolved and enlightened state of being were it not for the fact that even bugs know about gathering food stores for the whole colony or nest. What is enlightened in our case is not the action, but the choice to be at least as sensible as our insect friends and put our bodies to uses beyond themselves.

The body can function as a teacher as well, the sort of teacher you affectionately remember years afterward. "By indirections find directions out," advises Shakespeare's Polonius, and in such ways do the best of our teachers, including our own bodies, teach. If the New Testament has it right, feeling compassion, *splachnizomai*, originates not in the head or even the heart, but in the *splachna*, the gut. In other words, our bodies go before us in loving, and so teach the rest of us—mind and heart, that is—how it's done. Similarly, when we subject our bodies to a discipline such as fasting or exercise, the practice is training us indirectly for applying that discipline to our interior lives.

As the years leave their mark, our bodies continue to teach. In the circumstance of aging, we have the choice to begin to dismiss or even loathe our bodies. Instead, the body can teach us another way. When, as we begin to falter, we tend and care for ourselves with grace and good humor, our frumpier body is doing us the inestimable favor of training us in unconditional love. Love myself well in this context, and I will be more adept at offering the same to the next body over, regardless of its appearance or abilities.

Susan Jacoby writes about harboring some insecurity as she grew increasingly aware of the toll the years were taking in her face. Should she do something to recover some of her youthful attractiveness—soften some of the lines, take out some of the wrinkles? In other words, should she let surgical science lend a hand? As it turns out, someone else lent a hand first. As she tells it, the man in her life picked up on her facial fretting. He "placed his hands lightly on my temples, stepped back a half-pace and said, 'Your face is dear to me.'" Love doesn't give much better instruction than that.

Finally, drawing from the words of the apostle Paul, the body is often regarded as "a temple of the Holy Spirit, within you . . ." (1 Corinthians 6:19). This is all well and good, except for the fact that, as you know, the Holy Spirit is social by nature, which suggests our bodies might get crowded in a hurry. Imagine it: senior adults, children, youth, our peers—all represented inside of us, all metaphysically a part of us. This must be what Paul means when, backing up a few verses from the temple-of-the-Holy Spirit idea, he writes that "your bodies are members of Christ" (1 Corinthians 6:15).

Besides that crowd "inside" watching every move we make and being affected by it, in every Christian temple there is a baptismal font, a table of Eucharist, a Bible, some singing, some preaching, some praying, and, God willing, some experiencing new life—all happening right inside your body! Wow—who knew?

What we do with our bodies, we essentially do to *the* body—of Christ, that is. If I am neglectful of my body, you will feel it—and not just in your pocketbook when the cost of health care skyrockets. If, on the other hand, I offer myself in the service of Christ, the entire church is fortified. John Donne said in one of his sermons that no one is an island, entire of itself. He most probably took his cue from Corinthians.

People may wonder why we care for our bodies but without indulging them; why we let them teach us as though they had a head on their shoulders, why we are eager to make use of them for helping others, getting work done, bringing good news, praising God. Others may also wonder about the "temple" thing, housing the Holy Spirit and a billion of its closest friends. But over time they will begin to see; the temple will begin, more and more, to show through. As we age into frumpiness, becoming coats on a stick shuffling closer to the edge of the mortal coil, there may be less fire in our eyes but there will be more light, less pep in our step but greater purpose, more valves and stents and gizmos housed in our hearts but more love, too, and fewer regrets. Temples, as it turns out, age pretty well.

Chapter 9

Holding Lightly

*One must be light, with light heart and light hands—hold
and possess, hold and let go.*
From *Der Rosenkavalier*

The sixteenth century reformer Martin Luther once
remarked that God divided the hands into fingers so that
money could slip through. I don't think he saw this as a liabil-
ity but was speaking rather to a basic human longing—the
desire to do good, to help others, to share our resources with
those in need and so make a just and compassionate difference
in the world. Money, as we know, when put to such purposes
has historically accomplished precisely these sorts of things in
lives and communities. When, either through conviction or
vision or both, people determine to better the world around
them by financial means, the results can be inspiring. A hospital is built; a refugee family is housed and employed; water
wells are dug; a cathedral is constructed; an after-school pro-
gram is created; the hungry are fed; the gospel is shared; the
Word becomes flesh.

These undertakings are all ways of addressing our own longings—longings of the sort we spoke about previously, and of
the sort prophets have reminded us and remind us still—for
God's name to be uninjured, for the world to be reconciled, for

every human being to have access to basic necessities. The sharing of wealth can certainly allow some of these longings to find meaningful expression. But there is one other longing we considered before—the longing for enough to be enough. Luther's theory that fingers serve the purpose of helping us part with money is not only about caring for the world in its manifold needs but also about responding to a conviction or vision of another sort: the vision of living our lives free of the enslaving love of money. After all, we need our hands for other things, too. Open fingers help us meet a basic challenge that Jesus placed upon the lives of those who would know and follow him: you cannot serve both God and money; you are sure to love one and hate the other.

The notion of open fingers suggests that we aren't merely morally obligated to share our wealth for the sake of others or for the good of our own souls; we are genetically engineered to do so. To be human in the best sense is to let some things slip away—*on purpose*; it is to release what becomes too much for the benefit of others and, more to the point, ourselves.

Enter a small anatomical development that holds the whole money-through-the-fingers thing in an intriguing balance. Besides having fingers through which money slips, the human hand is endowed with another distinctive feature—opposable digits—that can have precisely the opposite effect. You know as well as I do what we can do with those handy-dandy, God-given thumbs: grab and grasp, clutch and cling. Where would we be without them? Certainly not on the jungle gym.

If money slips through fingers on the one hand, it is held fast on the other. Resting on the same hand, never far from one another, are that opposable thumb and those permeable fingers, so poised yet so precarious, each to the other both friend and nemesis. The hand, in other words, presents a perfect picture of the privileges and challenges of relating well to money. We are all of us contradictory creatures—eager by appetite to acquire more and more, but also longing for opportunities in which acquisition might take a back seat to something deeper—something like gratitude, compassion, or reverence. As much as we may want certain things for ourselves, we also yearn to experience the privilege of contributing a share of our wealth for some greater good, or simply to honor God. Such is our lot—made with the sure-fire capacity for securing enough, but also with the nimble ability to part with what becomes too much. The psalmist had it right—we are wonderfully made.

In some exquisite balance most of us are still working hard to achieve, we live in part to acquire, in part to give. Living in eighteenth-century England, John Wesley possessed a remarkable vision for the winning possibilities of that balance. He sought to honor the dual reality of our natural inclinations both to secure and to share. In his instruction to an up-and-coming middle class that was quickly learning not only how to devote themselves to God but also how to turn a nice profit, he used what has come to be regarded as a trademark of Methodism: the good old both-and approach. Lighting a candle to that magnificently acquisitive thumb, he advised them to "make all you can, and save all you can." Then, in a move that shouldn't surprise us, but usually does anyway, he lights another candle to those fingers through which money can so easily slip, telling his hearers to "give all they can." Make all you can. Save all you can. Give all you can.

What is so remarkable about John Wesley's perspective is that he's not asking for the world. He simply challenges the people of God to exert a reasonable effort, which then grows into a disciplined lifestyle, to share some of what we earn, not every dime and dollar, just what we can. Begin, he says, with putting your skills to earning big and saving well. *Then* ask the crucial question, and turn it into an adventure—or even a calling: what do I really need to set aside for myself and my family, and how much can I possibly afford to give away? In other words, what is the minimum I can afford to live on and the most I can afford to share? In Wesley's case, what remained in that equation for him to keep for himself turned out to be, by the time of his death, about four English pounds and a few books. He even left instructions that the crepe hanging at his funeral should subsequently be made into dresses to be given to the poor. In fulfilling his own vision of earn-save-give, he had succeeded.

Wesley seemed to understand what Luther also knew. They were, after all, both reading from the same book—the one that tells of our being crafted with both permeable fingers and opposable thumbs. Their listeners needed desperately to hear and heed a certain message: the more they kept, in the sense of hoarding, for the purpose of padding their nests, the narrower and shallower their spiritual lives would grow. However, the more they gave to God's purposes in the world, the wider and deeper their lives and witness before God and the world would become. *They*, incidentally, have become *us*. Along those same lines, *us* includes *you*.

Chapter 10

Regarding Words

Let your words proceed from silence . . .
Fred Craddock

T hink of the number of words that have found their way to
your eye or ear since your day began. For some of us, that
calculation would be virtually impossible to complete. We have
listened to far too many minutes of radio, TV, recorded music,
or conversation, or read too many Web pages, e-mails, news-
paper headlines, cereal boxes, street signs, or nutrition labels to
hazard even the wildest guess. We should remember to include
the words we see by way of wearing the brands of commerce on
our own bodies—caps, ties, jeans, shirts, shoes, purses, glasses,
watches, and the like. Add to the number count the labels on
the cars we drive, the pens we hold, the packages and contain-
ers carrying the food and drink we consume between words.

Words are the worker bees of human communication and
commerce, and they are legion. From flower to flower—mouth
to ear, print to eye—they move by the millions to carry the fer-
tilizing pollen of messages and their meanings. In this book
alone there are somewhere on the order of twenty-six thousand
such worker bees, in *War and Peace* perhaps ten times that
many. Then there are the countless habitats beyond the printed
page where the goods and services of words are rendered—on

billboards, candy wrappers, rubber stamps, radio waves, personal music devices, computer screens, clothes, nail clippers, livestock, skin, and of course, the tips of our tongues. Words are carved into trees, shaved into scalps, sung in arias, painted in caves, whispered across pillows, displayed from rooftops, thumbed into text messages, spelled by trick planes, and coaxed into formation in verbose bowls of alphabet soup.

By and large, words are up to the task of filling our mouths, eyes, ears, brains, hearts, planet, and beyond to the point of utter and complete saturation. Work them as hard as we may, they remain in the line of duty, never once second-guessing our intentions any more than a worker bee questions the queen. They take on a message and carry it elsewhere, then another, then another. By their labors they hearten, insult, bless, curse, cajole, inform, woo, frighten, wound, and heal. They inspire, defame, confuse, enlighten, caress, embattle, and soothe. For dirty deeds and noble ones, done dirt cheap, words are at your service.

What happens, however, when there are so many words doing so many deeds that no longer can any single word be heard? How often have you felt that way—that your words were falling on ears that were not listening? Or that the sleeve-tugging interruptions by little ones have elicited only a vague response from you, because your own ears or mind were otherwise occupied? *"My wife says I never listen to her—or something like that,"* reads the bumper sticker. Perhaps it was merely a statement of fact—the insurance is due; the gutters need cleaning. Or was a sentiment being expressed? Were there words beneath the spoken words, a question behind the comment? Was the person seeking something more than a momentary exchange of information, perhaps some encouragement, some comfort, some understanding? OK, then, if that's the case, let's set everything aside and talk for a minute or two—oh—hold on a second—I really need to take this call . . .

With continuous partial attention we half-listen as others speak, speak as others half-listen, interrupt and are interrupted at regular intervals, only marginally expecting to be understood or to offer understanding in any meaningful way. Meanwhile, words increase in number and pitch, vying for shrinking levels of attention; the precious, sense-making gift of meaningful verbal communication has been pushed to the furthest recesses of our day. This, I think, is what T. S. Eliot meant when he asked, "Where shall the word be found, where will the word / Resound? Not here, there is not enough silence."

I was recently in a place where there *was* enough silence for the word to resound. It was the stroke recovery wing of a rehabilitation center. The woman I visited, Mrs. Dale, had been seriously debilitated by a stroke months before and was essentially without sequential speech. She could generate a word here or there—perhaps two; that was all. In terms of meaningful verbal communication, her body had been her prison cell for nearly half a year. You wouldn't know it from her buoyant face, her warm smile. As I walked into Mrs. Dale's room and crouched by her wheelchair, I began some introductory one-way conversation with her, then tapered to silence to allow myself to be quiet in her presence, and she in mine.

After some time, it was clear she wanted to say something. She began to shape her mouth, focus her bright eyes, lean her head slightly forward. She spent what seemed like an eternity working, laboring, struggling to bring her thoughts to speech. I waited, patiently at first, then less so, looking into her earnest gaze as she worked her mouth and facial muscles toward that activity that comes to most of us like breathing. More than once I nearly interrupted her feeble efforts to speak by supplying filler words of my own, but then, thinking better of it, kept silent. On she worked, the deep-sea diver silently searching the ocean depths for that pendant, that coin, that pearl of great price, until finally she broke the water's surface, treasure in hand. In a mere whisper of a breath, she spoke the single word for which she had been so desperately reaching. "Hope," she said. That was all.

After receiving that single pearl at once so mystifying and so beautiful, and praying whatever brief prayer I could muster, I left Mrs. Dale's room in silence, but her room didn't leave me. For the longest while, I could only hear her word, in her voice. I made a picture in my mind of how that word came to speech inside her. Shoulder on shoulder all the muted words had climbed, until they stood tall enough to reach the barred window of the prison cell her body had become. Once there, their chosen messenger—the only word that had somehow received special powers of clemency—climbed to the top of the word ladder to press against the bars and speak. "Hope."

"Our words are wiser than we are," a poet once told Kathleen Norris. If that is so, then I wonder what wisdom our words would offer if we were to allow ourselves the stillness to hear them speak, uninterrupted, for a brief time. They may prove reluctant to say anything at all. The modern world has been hemorrhaging words for quite some time, and they may want a mere moment's peace in an effort to regain their strength.

But once recovered, perhaps they would draw their breath and say, "We are free, but we are not cheap. Regard us well." Or, by way of reminding us that ratcheting up volume and pitch does not always serve us well, they might recall Søren Kierkegaard having said "Something true when whispered may become false when shouted."

They might speak of how, as words, they long to take part in the goodness in things, the tenderness in things, the beginnings of things, the hope in things; how when the world was not, a thousand means were available to God to still the formless chaos and bring forth life, but for that purpose God chose *words. Let there be . . .* the words said as they emerged from the silence. *And there was.*

Remember, our words would say, the Word being made into flesh, full of grace and truth, who with a single word brought healing, or forgiveness, or bread, or hope, or even life itself. Remember all the ways and all the times since in which through Jesus' followers' own mature or makeshift deeds of grace and truth, the Word has continued to stutter its way into flesh. Craft your words with care, then, and offer them gently. Receive them from others as gate lamps to the world behind the face from which they come. By such means does God reveal glimpses of hearts and lives, glimpses of the new creation.

The words are organizing even as we speak. From within their prison cell, this one constructed not by a stroke, but by crowded airwaves, frenetic mouthways, and verbose highways, they are building their word ladder and sending that same utility player on a careful upward climb. It is a daring venture. Any moment the ladder could collapse—words are that fragile. But words are even more durable and daring than they are fragile, and so they brace themselves, flex and bend and shoulder the weight, helping their partner in that patient, determined climb. After all, that single word spoken is what lends courage to the rest, and, truth be told, to us as well. Up and up the word goes, finally reaching the barred window at the top, and offering itself as though nothing else mattered in the world, only this single pearl, raised from the depths into the light. "Hope."

Chapter 11

The Courage to Say No

Teach me the beauty of my emptiness.
Katherine Mosby

$\mathcal{J}$ ust say no," goes the popular slogan for a campaign to encourage youth to abstain from drugs. As if to say, it's that easy—one word and you're free of involvement in something you shouldn't be doing. If someone wants you to take that illicit step with them, then all you need to do is follow these simple directions: (1) Draw your breath just slightly; (2) press your tongue to the roof of your mouth; (3) begin to speak, dropping your tongue and rounding your lips as you do. Congratulations— in three easy steps you have just said no!

Who are we kidding? There is nothing easy about saying no— whether it's to drugs or doughnuts with sprinkles. If it's a dress we don't need, an overture from beyond the boundaries, a shady business proposition, or even a good thing at the wrong time —saying no is no piece of cake. To deny an opportunity to satisfy ourselves in some way—legal or otherwise—can be an extremely difficult task. Just ask anyone who has attempted to observe even the simplest Lenten abstinence or lose a few pounds for health reasons. Add the fact that, when it comes to appetite or opportunity, yes is our cultural mantra, and saying no just became that much more difficult.

Adding one further layer of complexity, a layer that will probably meet most of us right about eye level, restraint is not only about avoiding things of questionable moral value—late night rendezvous in abandoned warehouse districts, clandestine requests by *mafiosi* in dark glasses to launder their millions—that sort of thing. Sometimes no must be said to good things that are not the best things—one more activity for us or our children, one more promotion at work, one more improvement for our home, one more vacation, one more . . .

You finish the sentence, because only you know what those things are in your life. They're good things all, and if you did say yes to them and were then asked why you made such a choice, you could justify yourself up one side and down the other. In fact, the one who asked would more than likely help you with the answers: It's a good investment. It secures my family's future. It gives the children all the opportunities we want for them. I've been working so hard lately. I deserve this. It's a good value. It will last for years. I couldn't refuse. There's no one else who could do it. All of these are good reasons for filling our lives with possessions, status, activities, and responsibilities. Yet if these "additions" lead us away from "walking modestly with our God"—offering much, but needing little—then what have we lost in the bargain?

Sometimes modesty even involves saying no simply to allow for a dimension of vacancy, or breathing room, in our lives. Availability is a rare commodity in our time. Meanwhile, "I'm busy" has become the gold standard for self-importance. No one wishes to be "embarrassingly available," as my late colleague Wil Bailey used to describe himself. Busy, on the other hand, conveys a sense of significance, as though we and our wall-to-wall activities were actually essential to the running of the world. We'll look more a few chapters over at the art of finding balance in our lives between work and Sabbath. For now, I am reminded of Fred Craddock's observation, drawn from Goethe: "It is the nature of grace that it can only enter empty spaces." To say no to certain things—not just "drugs" but good things as well—is to allow for clearings in our thickly settled calendars into which grace might enter, and from which new life may emerge.

Have you ever felt hemmed in by all the yeses you feel obligated to say? Have you wished at times to say no, but lacked the freedom or confidence to do so? How do we come to that place of freedom and confidence? What enables us to choose *not* instead of *to*? How are we to manage to lift our tongue and round our lips instead of open wide our mouth, given the world's gravitational pull toward the latter?

Jesus shows us a way. He has just been baptized and is being led by the Holy Spirit into the wilderness of Judea (Luke 4). Whether the devil has found his address or he the devil's, we can't be sure. In any event, in the encounter two worlds collide. One world views expediency as paramount; the other, faithfulness. The first world ends at the borders of my own skin; the second acknowledges a universe beyond.

The conversation that gives voice to these two worldviews is remarkably near to the conversations that go on in our own heads, and swirl around them, on a daily basis. Devil: "You deserve a break today—get what you want the easy way." Jesus: "Getting what you want is thin soup compared to being nourished in relationship to God and God's teachings about the best way to live." Devil: "Your powers of devotion are a commodity, and like any other, they can be traded." Jesus: "Whether they are tradable or not, God is the one true focus of our devotion." Devil: "How can you be sure God really loves you unless you insist on proof?" Jesus: "Some things are true beyond the realm of proving."

They say the devil is in the details. The opposite may be closer to the truth. It is generalizations that tend to win crowds, whereas details often put them to sleep. Every assertion, every promise the devil offers is a broad-stroke gloss, the fine print conveniently missing from the page. Popular folk wisdom in the form of favorite Scripture verses is turned sideways in an effort to justify everything but faith. The devil has been reading Emily Dickinson: *Tell all the truth, but tell it slant.*

Jesus faced a resistance that had all the backing of the common world behind it and he went another way. How do we do the same? How do we negate the worldview that locates the center of the world inside of me? How do we say no to that which we don't need, isn't right, would betray some promise, or is simply too much of a good thing—especially when the whole world has given its blessing, or even expects compliance? I only know one way—the same way Jesus did so: in the company of courage.

When Jesus reached the desert's edge, not only was he still wet behind the ears from his baptism at the hands of his cousin John, not only were the words of his heavenly Father still close on his ear, not only had the Holy Spirit descended upon him in baptism and now ushered him into the wilderness; one other dimension is so obvious as to escape notice. In between Jesus' baptism and the wilderness, we are given a list of sorts—a genealogy. It is the sort of thing we tend to read if we're having trouble falling asleep. In this instance, however, the genealogy serves as a *tour de force* demonstration of how to confront difficult choices. Not only does Jesus have his cousin John, the Holy Spirit, and the Father's love, he has generations of family lined up behind him. All of this makes for a rather well-populated wilderness. If the world is larger than my own skin's boundaries, then so are the resources by which I can successfully navigate through it.

Courage, as it turns out, finds its clearest voice in the company of others. If we are to say no, then it must be *we* who say no—I in the awareness of God, Jesus, the Spirit, my baptism, and a community of courage whose stories of good choices precede my own. This community not only helps us say no but just as important, helps us discern when no is the right answer in the first place—inherited counsel we could never summon in isolation. John Ames's words in the novel *Gilead* speak to that reality: "Theologians talk about a prevenient grace that precedes grace itself and allows us to accept it. I think there must also be a prevenient courage that allows us to be brave. . . ." There is, indeed—it is the courage of our mothers, fathers, teachers, friends, heroes ancient and modern—all those who, visibly or invisibly, walk with us into the various choice-making wildernesses of our lives and lend us their courage for summoning our own, in order to speak the word often so very difficult to say alone: No.

part three

The Good Work

My work be praise.

Isaac Watts

Chapter 12

Usefulness

To be useful was the best thing the old men ever hoped for themselves, and to be aimless was their worst fear.
Marilynne Robinson, *Gilead*

*W*hy do you work? You would think such a question would have a simple answer. And yet, get up close to the question, and it turns out there are a dozen different answers, a hundred different reasons we work—none of them simply put. To put bread on the table? To do something you really enjoy? To make a name for yourself or a difference in the world? To get out of the house? To maintain a certain standard of living? To achieve financial security? To be around people you like? To fulfill a need to serve others? To follow what you would say is God's leading or direction in your life?

Maybe you work because you feel stuck in a certain job or role, or in a certain income/expense bracket, and see no reasonable way out, so you stay on the treadmill. Perhaps you're living out what Graham Greene calls the "long despair of doing nothing well," and in each day's effort is hidden the feeble hope that this may be the day you finally get it right. It could be that one reason you work is because long ago people told you that you would never amount to anything, and you've since been trying to prove them wrong. Or the reverse may be true—

someone told you that if you worked hard you *could* make it in life, and you've kept your eyes on that prize ever since.

Some of us might say we regard work in the same way a sick child regards the medicine in a spoon—as an unfortunate means of achieving a desired outcome. I once attended a worship service honoring the theologian Elisabeth Schüssler Fiorenza that ended with a spirited version of the song "Freedom Is Coming."

> *Freedom is coming.*
> *Freedom is coming, oh yes, I know.*

The singing broke into dancing as the leaders of worship stepped and swayed up the aisle, and those of us in the pews clapped and swayed with them, thoroughly enjoying the festive beat. It was then I noticed a woman near the front, *very* pregnant, and appearing *very* ready to be delivered of her precious cargo. She was patting the underside of her large belly to the beat of the song as she quietly swayed and sang, *Freedom is coming, oh yes, I know.* Sometimes work's most immediate significance for us is that "this, too, shall pass." Whether it's a very pregnant belly, a volunteer assignment, a work project, or even a career, we'll be more satisfied with the end than we are with the means, and the sooner the better.

But why do *you* work? In the home, outside the home, as a volunteer, for pay, rearing children or raising profit margins, doing the taxes or the dishes, carrying out a business deal or the trash, nursing a night shift or a baby? Among the many things that motivate us to work, one must surely be that, simply put, there's work to be done, and we believe that what we do is meeting a need, directly or indirectly, of something or someone other than ourselves.

Maybe Adam works the ground by the sweat of his brow because by digging around in the very dirt from which he came he might somehow "find himself," but there are also mouths to feed. Eve may understand the travail of childbirth partly as having something to do with paradise lost, but the fact is a baby needs birthing, and it will need some help getting there. We work, at least in part, because someone else needs us to, a plain obligation that tends to reduce our own self-centeredness to manageable dimensions. Now we are important not because we're all that, but because, as James Taylor once put it, "baby's hungry and the money's all gone."

If we see work as being about usefulness, the rewards of such a view can be slow in coming, but tend to run deep. In A. J. Verdelle's novel, *The Good Negress*, a wise, matronly grandmother offers her granddaughter, who is devastated to learn that her mother has abandoned her, some sturdy counsel for moving on from her temple of hurt feelings. She says, "The best way to make y'self feel better is to get y'hands to workin. When you put y'hands on somethin and make it somethin else, that will heal you lower places that you cry from."

The poignancy of the grandmother's insight is that there are hurts within us we cannot touch with our own two hands, let alone repair, hurts that originate in places even lower than we cry from. The only way those places get healed is by training our hands in other directions. In the grandmother's recipe, healing comes through handiwork, taking a thing and making it into something else. In her world, as the granddaughter will soon learn, that translates into keeping house—clothing and feeding and cleaning up after the hodgepodge of family that makes a home under Granmama's roof.

Henri Nouwen gave us the notion of the "wounded healer" in his book of the same name, suggesting that there are many times when our work is carried out in the midst of personal loss, longing, or brokenness, so that the work itself becomes a salve to our own hearts even as it offers something to another. In *Evensong* Gail Godwin refers to one of her characters, a plaintive priest, as living "by the grace of daily obligation." The phrase suggests that somehow the practice of moving out of ourselves for the sake of doing what is needed has the power to become a means of grace, giving life to our own wearied souls.

But we needn't be wounded or melancholy to have a need to be useful. The urge is universal, meaning the confident and self-possessed feel it too. Barbara Kingsolver suggests in *Small Wonder* that there is within all of us an "intimate connection between the will to survive and the need to feel useful to something or someone beyond myself." If the first thing we do as newborns fresh out of the chute is draw a desperate breath to jump-start a sticky pair of lungs, then a close second is to wail looks of sheer wonder onto the faces of everyone present, and especially two people in particular. Wonder, when you think about it, is one of the most useful experiences to which we can ever introduce another person, and here we are making that contribution from the get-go, owing to the simple fact that we needed to find a breath. That primal inhale/exhale moment pretty much sets the rhythm for life, wherein needing and giving are of a piece.

It would be wrong to suggest that because good work is inherently useful, then work is not about any of the other motives we mentioned above—of course it is—or that none of these other motives are legitimate—many of them are. Usefulness to others is more like a touchstone without which all the other reasons we work tend to grow threadbare with time. If we grow old without having given ourselves to others in any intentionally useful way, then we will have succeeded in deftly pulling a treasure chest up a great hill only to open the lid to discover that it holds a dull collection of rocks.

Francis of Assisi, born in the twelfth century to an Italian family eager to endow him with a life of ease and irrelevance, walked away from the chest he was expected to tote up the great hill and gave his life over instead to the pursuit of God, this by means of serving a needy world. He saw himself as a tool in God's hands and his own fulfillment all tied up in the fulfillment of others. In that spirit of usefulness to God and others, a prayer was written centuries later that bears Saint Francis's name. Who's to say that if we pray the prayer long enough and live it well enough, it might not come to bear ours too:

Lord, make me an instrument of thy peace. Where there is hatred, let me sow love; where there is injury, pardon; doubt, faith; despair, hope; darkness, light; sadness, joy. O Divine Master, grant that I may not so much seek to be consoled as to console, to be understood as to understand, to be loved as to love. For it is in giving that we receive, it is in pardoning that we are pardoned, it is in dying that we are born to eternal life.

Chapter 13

Purpose

The creature hath a purpose,
and its eyes are bright with it.
John Keats

A time comes in our lives when whatever we do for a living—
litigate, mow, keep house, clean, doctor, nurse, teach, sing,
rear young, pave streets, cook, tell stories, design, govern,
plumb, or compose—begs a question. Not the earlier question,
"Why do I work?" but a second one, related but also different:
"What does my work *do?*" The first question is about our own
reasons for doing whatever it is we do; the second is about ways
in which what we do affects in lasting ways the world around us.

The French philosopher Michel Foucault once put the matter in the form of a funny little word twist: "People know what
they do; they frequently know why they do what they do; but
what they don't know is what what they do does."

What Foucault has given us is a way to frame the question of
what happens after we decide we want to look beyond usefulness in our lives to purpose: what does what I do *do* for others
and the world? For a Christian particularly, the question
becomes sharpened in this way: can I do what I do in such a way
as to offer others and the world the gift that has been offered to
me—life abundant? Lending a hand is one thing, shaping a life

another. Give someone a fish, the old proverb goes, and they eat for a day. Teach them to fish, and they eat for a lifetime. From the first act to the second you have gone from being merely helpful to being life-transforming, a quantum shift in anybody's book.

Speaking of fish and fishing, Jesus once framed the whole matter of purposefulness in precisely those terms. At the risk of lingering too long with a smelly subject—hold your nose for a minute—walking by the Sea of Galilee, Jesus called some fishermen in from their work (useful work it was—feeding their families, employing day laborers, quality time on the boat with Dad) and offered them work of a different sort. "From now on," he told them, "you will be fishing for people" (Mark 1:16-20, paraphrased).

I warned you to hold your nose. We all know how fish can smell, even in a metaphor. But there's another good reason this little illustration is unsavory to modern Western noses: the very idea of "fishing for people" is instinctively onerous to us. The presumption of Jesus to suggest that these new followers should go around netting new converts, hooking new believers, bait-trapping new followers offends us to the gills. Ours is a society founded upon respect and regard for individual rights and liberties; and whatever that meant at the time of the founding (and it did mean something quite a bit more nuanced than we generally suppose), the generations-long process of filtering this idea through a philosophical sieve of individualism, privatism, and relativism has thinned out its meaning considerably. We are, you and I, the children of a pop culture that has come to hold individual self-determination as virtually sacrosanct. To borrow a lyric from the seventies that, conveniently suspending for its purposes the self-determination-as-sacrosanct dogma, found its way countless times into many of our ears whether we wanted it to or not, "It's your thing, do what you wanna do. I can't tell you who to sock it to."

How can we bring the fishing invitation of Jesus into our time and culture when it appears to violate our ramped-up notions of individual freedom and self-determination? If having a sense of purpose in my life means snagging people with 100-pound mono line and a hot pink Ballyhoo lure, I'll stick with usefulness and leave purpose to others. What is a person of faith to do?

Turn the page, that's what. Not *this* page—the page in the Bible that has Jesus calling these followers to fish for people. When we do so, we immediately discover that Jesus means something rather different by that phrase. Within casting distance of his invitation, he heals a man with an unclean spirit, the mother-in-law of one of the fishermen, many others who were sick with various diseases, a leper, and a paralytic (see Mark 1 and 2). After being healed—this will be startling to some, as it was to me—*those who are healed are not heard from again*. These fish are not being caught in a net, but the opposite: released from nets in which they've long been entangled, darting away into the anonymous deep.

When Jesus speaks of fishing for people, he doesn't mean *catching* them. In these instances, through the gift of healing, he means *setting them free*. Self-determination is not compromised by the ministry of Jesus and his followers; on the contrary, it is awakened! "Power came out from him and healed all of them," Luke writes in summary fashion (6:19), further defining purposeful living as the sharing of power with those who are weak, not for our benefit, but for theirs. We must believe these transfers of power, these untrapping experiences, brought some—perhaps many—eventually back to Jesus and his motley band. Even so, in the Gospels, when it comes to "fishing for people," it seems that the central point is not racking up numbers but freedom.

If you and I are to decide the step beyond useful to purposeful is one we want to take, then we will begin to ask ourselves, in our relationships with others, how can I invite this person or these persons to lives of greater freedom and power? How can I teach them to fish so they are released from the burden of returning daily for another portion of fish. How can I best introduce them to the open frontier of a relationship with the Nazarene who sets people free for a living? On the level of systems, such as the church and others who provide social services or advocate for the poor, how can I move from simply supporting the *status quo* to bringing a vision for more humane and faithful structures of care and well-being? In some instances, we will not so much do different things, or even do what we do differently, but *understand* more clearly "what what we do does." It is even possible that being freed from a "recruiting" mentality will allow us more fully to offer concern, compassion, friendship, a prophetic voice—whatever is called for that we have to offer.

A host of issues arises when we raise the subject of interesting others in our own spiritual experience and religious worldview, or talk about seeking to reform rather than merely maintain institutions that seek to aid those in need. We won't deal with those issues here, save one—the question of arrogance. For people of faith, the starting place for any intention to introduce a new idea or perspective to other individuals or systems must be our own humility. The mystery of how God works in lives and in the world is beyond us, which means one of the best ways to fish is by pointing: "There is a place I believe I have seen God at work." "Here inside myself I have recognized God's power to change a life." Pointing is different from coercing in the same way that setting free is different from catching. Whether as an individual, a church, or a society, we forget that difference to our own self-delusion and others' potential harm. When we remember it, however, we understand and live out our purpose as followers of this Jesus, who fished for people by setting them free. We are empowered to become all that God created us to be precisely through empowering others to become all that God created them to be. That's what I would call a fine kettle of fish.

Chapter 14

Transcendence

We knew not whether we were in heaven or on earth.

Royal emissaries reporting to
tenth-century Russian Prince Vladimir,
after visiting Hagia Sophia

*W*ork is about usefulness to something or someone other than ourselves. It eventually leads us into questions of purpose, where we begin to see our life's work in terms of transforming human lives and human institutions toward freedom and wholeness. Yet even though work is about usefulness and purpose, it is also very much about something else altogether: drawing near our Maker, having first awakened to the good news that our Maker has inexplicably drawn near to us. If the central dynamic of work is giving and receiving, then the work of worship is receiving the gift of life in God's presence and realm, and offering our thanks for the unspeakable wonder of such a gift. In this light, all our work becomes praise, and praise becomes our work. Or rather praise becomes the work of God through us, for there is far more to the work of worship than meets the eye. *Much water goeth by the mill that the miller knoweth not of,* John Heywood once observed. He could have been speaking of that mill we know of as the church at prayer.

Liturgy is a word often used to describe worship, and one of that word's root meanings is "the work of the people." The work of the people in worship can be defined and explored in many ways, one of which is in terms of "transcendence." Transcendence is the way we speak of a God who, as we mentioned in the previous chapter, is beyond us, shrouded in mystery. What happens when, in worship, we seek to draw near that mystery with eyes ready to behold, ears ready to listen, hearts ready to be surrendered? We are, ourselves, taken up into that same transcendence that describes the One who is the object of our worship.

The word *transcend* means literally "to climb across," and expresses something of the ascending and migrating that happen when worship is true to its sources. We begin with words, music, songs, prayers, water, bread, cup—familiar tools and idioms from our common life. By the end of it all, however, we have been somewhere other than the "familiar" places of our common life; we have "climbed across," been transported, as it were, to another realm, and back again. There may even be moments in that journey into the numinous in which we can "scarcely tell whether we are in heaven or on earth." But the journey happens regardless of what we sense or feel, imagine or contemplate, whether we "get something out of it" or not. As with so many other things in life, worship is not primarily about *feeling* what we do, but *meaning* what we do. As my teacher Don Saliers would say, the deep emotions of the faith are not a matter of what strikes our fancy in a given moment of scintillating worship, but what forms our hearts over the long-ranging practices and rhythms of communal prayer and life.

As a child I spent summers with my family at my grandparents' home in rural Oklahoma, which is where I first came to know Mrs. Grace Nuner. Every Sunday we attended a small church in the nearby town, where often as not the four of us children were the only youngsters in the place. When it could be arranged, we would have a makeshift Sunday school lesson, then gather with the grown-ups for worship. There were no "words with children" in the middle of the service, no children's church in a separate wing—we were right there in the small-frame sanctuary with God and everybody, and in it for the long haul. It was there that Mrs. Nuner grew to become larger than life in the eyes of four Escamilla children—my sister, my two brothers, and myself. Sitting next to us in the pew as the service began, she played a role I did not begin to understand until years later, and in a very real way, don't yet.

After a hymn or two was sung, prayers offered, the offering taken, and Scripture read, the sermon would commence. Now you know as well as I do that a sermon is the mischief in many a child, and we were no exception. There was great opportunity in this moment, and now was the time to put our heads together and see what could be devised. It was then Mrs. Nuner, with the instincts of a mother bird, would quietly move into action. Sitting next to us, she would reach out her open hand, and one of us would offer her our bulletin. She would take it and begin slowly and painstakingly to transform it from a folded piece of paper with mimeographed words on the inside and perhaps a Cokesbury Jesus on the cover into the most magnificent paper airplane you've ever seen. We were transfixed at every turn—the slight tearing of the paper here, folding it there, pressing to a crease, opening to a wing. When she was done, she would hand her creation to the lucky first-chosen, receive the next paper offering from the next child, and repeat the miracle.

What we witnessed, and at eye level, was that worship is a crafted vessel. We furnish raw materials of the most ordinary sort—in this case a flight manual—and these are drawn up, made flightworthy, flown elsewhere, then offered back, along with their occupants, at once the same and utterly changed. Jesus told the disciples to go and prepare a meal, and by nightfall, with their simple provisions in his hands, he had taken them lands away. *Take and eat . . . Drink from this, all of you . . .*

Grace Nuner's airplanes were not your ordinary stock productions—fold a sheet of paper in half, crease an angled wing, then another, maybe blunt the nose, and you've got your aircraft; that was our level. Mrs. Nuner worked in a higher realm; her creations were virtual works of art, and her making of them, poetry in motion. Curiously, just about the time the last airplane was being quietly placed into the fourth pair of waiting hands, the sermon would be winding down, the closing hymn sung, the benediction given. As we received the sending forth from the preacher, we held in hand, each of us, a token of the hour's work and wonder—that by some grace beyond our deserving, we had gone somewhere extraordinary and then returned, all in an hour's time, an out-and-back rapture right there on the fourth pew, right-hand side. Four little stair-step novices and one fully grown navigator, touring the ineffable.

Martin Buber once wrote that every journey has a secret destination of which the traveler is unaware. When we enter the time and place of worship, even those who preside, who organize the words, the music, the stories, the silence, are not able to say or know just where the "climbing across" will lead, and how it will leave us when we are set back down in the original place. Even the paper in our hands or images on a screen from which we take our cues are subject to transformation. What we can be certain of is that, if we are open to the journey—and sometimes even if we are not—we will come back changed, and with a silencing awareness that we have been somewhere besides here, met someone besides each other, touched and handled things unseen, encountered a presence bigger than all of us, and, most fortunate of all, lived to tell about it. The idea is that, having briefly seen the world in a different way, we will now, well, see the world in a different way.

Chapter 15

Rest

And on the seventh day, God finished the work that he
had done, and he rested . . .
G e n e s i s   2 : 2

Good work is the centerpiece of our lives, calling us in myriad ways over our lifetimes to seek usefulness, purpose,
and transcendence as ways of expressing our innate need to
reach beyond ourselves to meet needs, impart life to others,
and encounter God. But is work all we do? Is the drumbeat
calling us to reach beyond ourselves one that never ceases?
Sewn into the fabric of work are two rather ephemeral strands,
rest and play, two threads without which even good work
becomes the thinnest of blankets. We'll ease our way into the
first of these elements, rest, before, in the chapter that follows,
breaking for recess.

The concept of rest, or Sabbath, brings to the fore once
again something we looked at briefly in the first chapter of this
book: the unseemly notion that God is modest in both character and attributes. The Genesis creation story paints a portrait
of the Divine at first hard at work, then suddenly stopping—
to rest. Just to clarify, this is the Sovereign of the universe
we're talking about, the Creator of all that exists, the God who
was and is and is to come, who speaks and the world comes to

be. The One who breathes and life is born is all of a sudden taking a breather. The very idea may astound us, baffle us, or amuse us; mostly, I think it is so far-fetched it simply escapes our notice.

The modesty implicit both on the narrator's part for relating the story in such a way and in the image of God conveyed by the story continues to intrigue me. The pressure to portray God otherwise, as *way beyond* any desire or need for resting, would be immense. We like our deities not just heroic, but indefatigable besides. We prefer our public leaders Teflon tough, our pastors inexhaustible, our doctors mythic, our sports figures Herculean. If God is going to fit in with our society's standard for champions, then 24/7 at-the-ready high-performance is a fundamental expectation. Winners never quit, champions never give up, and leaders never rest. Rest is for the faint of heart. Time off is for the lazy. Sabbath is for the weak.

A billboard advertisement for a hospital's emergency room says it all. In the background is a picture of planets orbiting in space, and in the foreground, these words: *And on the seventh day, he rested . . . We don't.* We've come a long way since Genesis, having acquired the ability to outwork God.

In apparent contrast to God, we seem to hold up famously to a seven-day workweek. Or do we? OK, so we don't know all the sources and causes of stress, strain, creative drain, fatigue, depression, anxiety, insomnia, heart disease, hypertension, diabetes, eating disorders, or any of a host of other illnesses; only that overwork is a common suspect. Nor can we calculate the way in which a best-never-rest understanding of life has shaped philosophies of enterprise, theories of economic growth, politics of expansion and domination, and theologies of church growth and works righteousness.

What we do know, indisputably, is that bothersome little fact that won't stop reinserting itself into our discussion: God rested. Later on in the biblical narrative, Moses rolls out a commandment that says that we shall rest too. It's a commandment to which we've paid about as much attention as we have to the idea of God resting—which is to say, not much.

Four things happen when God chooses to rest and the biblical narrator chooses to tell us about it. First, a sense of trust is revealed in God's nature, what Wendell Berry has called "unconcern." It is as if God were saying, "I'm not worried about the work I've done falling into ruin, sliding into the sea, vaporizing into oblivion. My work stands or falls on its own; it will be what it will be, just as *I am that I am.* Therefore, I can afford to leave off working when I choose."

Rest is what we do when we trust that forces greater than our own are circulating in the world, "silently working for good." To practice Sabbath, or rest time, is to entrust our good work to the care of others. It is to rehearse for all the letting-go moments of our lives, including that final letting-go moment, when the shadows lengthen and the busy world is hushed, and our reach no longer extends far and wide, managing, as we imagine, whole worlds at a time, but only as far as the hand of the one who stands over our bed, and must be trusted to carry on without us from here.

Secondly, there is a sense of closure in the portrayal of God's resting. "God finished the work . . . and he rested . . ." the passage reads, suggesting that resting is a demarcation of a job completed, a purpose fulfilled. When is the last time you rested after a job well done, rather than hurrying on to the next task? To be present to our own finished work, taking time to linger with a certain regard, almost as a signature to that completed task, is an art as shaky in our time as cursive writing. Rest, in this sense, allows for duly honoring one effort before we move to another.

A third dynamic of God's rest is that God may have simply been tuckered out, and needed a little time to knit up "the ravelled sleeve of care," as Shakespeare put it. To practice Sabbath is to resist the powerful current of society that esteems tired-ness—like busyness—as a badge of self-importance. Instead of allowing for the natural remedy of rest, we often court our tiredness with caffeine and other performance-enhancing drugs. This is the tacit agreement worker makes with worker, boss with laborer, scholar with student, parish with priest that we shall all work harder, longer, faster, focusing our beefed-up energies around earning our own worth, and resisting any need for grace and freedom.

More about freedom in a minute. For the moment, grace. The monastic tradition gifts us with a communal view of the world from a world removed, a view that considers in the light of God's grace both the goodness and harshness of which we're humanly capable. From that tradition comes this tender story:

> Some old men came to Abba Poemen and said to him, "We see some of the brothers falling asleep during divine worship. Should we wake them?" He said, "As for me, when I see a brother who is falling asleep during the Office, I lay his head on my knees and let him rest."

When shall we let each other rest? How long shall we collec-tively refuse to listen to our ever-compliant bodies whisper to us their plea for a break from the driven pace of modern life? Allow me to be bored, to drift off for a moment or several, to consider the world sluggish on occasion rather than pencil-sharp. Allow me, please, to rest. It was good enough for God.

Freedom, as a reason to rest, waits until last, for it unleashes a subversive power that could empty the factory in a heartbeat. God rested on the seventh day because God *could* rest on the seventh day; it was within God's sovereign freedom and power to do so. Later on, when God's people were told they *would* rest on the Sabbath, it was in part to remind them of a time in their lives, their history, when they couldn't. Not on the Sabbath; not ever. They were slaves in Egypt and were worked long and hard, requiring permission even to breathe. (If you think I'm exaggerating, recall the time their newborn children were denied even breath.) To observe Sabbath in the time of freedom is a religious manifesto of body and soul: *I am not a slave, either to you or to myself, though I remember keenly that I and my kind once were. By the power and grace of God to deliver a people through wave and wilderness, I am free.* Resting is our passive but militant pledge that never again will we either be enslaved, enslave ourselves, or inflict such inhumanity on any other.

In more ways than we can know, rest is an essential part of the rhythm of life, allowing us to experience trust, completion, grace, and freedom. When we practice rest in deliberate and welcoming ways, we acknowledge that we are not everything, nor do we need to be. We could claim that such a modest view of things is original to us, were it not for God.

Chapter 16

Play

A garden requires much work,
but sometimes it just needs enjoying.
Lee May, *In My Father's Garden*

*A*s a child I enjoyed the special attentions of my Tio Gregorio, my Uncle Greg, around a little rhyme he taught me because it included my name in its word play: *Pablito clavó un clavito. Un clavito clavó Pablito.* The English translation does not allow quite the grammatical reflexivity, or mirroring, of the Spanish, but it still conveys the gist of the doublet: *Paul nailed a nail. A nail nailed Paul.* English's closest parallel is probably *Peter Piper picked a peck of pickled peppers. If Peter Piper picked a peck of pickled peppers, then how many pickled peppers did Peter Piper pick?*

Notice how with both Pablito and Peter work turns to play as the subject at hand, hammering a nail or picking a crop, is described with whimsical word and speech patterns. Then, conversely, play turns to work as the challenge of vocalizing the silly rhyme calls forth mental focus and verbal effort beyond what conveying the simple facts would require. As you know, "Peter Piper" is intended to be repeated three times fast, or five, or ten, to provide the full effect of a twisted tongue. But why? Don't we have enough to do without taxing our brain and twisting our tongue for the sake of reporting in on someone else's work habits?

What these rhymes and a thousand like them illustrate is that work and play are not opposites as we often suppose, but a dance pair. Play takes work, and on a good day work involves an element of play as well. Play seasons a life engaged in usefulness, purpose, transcendence, and rest. And that seasoning somehow opens up possibilities for living our lives in greater balance, creativity, and reverence.

Children warm to play by nature, learning laughter long before they learn speech. They will splash the bath water, hum a meandering tune, kick a stone down the street to nowhere in particular. In these instances, it is not work that calls for the mitigating or infusing qualities of play, but play that reveals a young child's non-instrumental world—the inborn instinct to do a thing just to do a thing. It is a world to which, as we grow older, we return only through a state of grace. Worship, as we've already seen, is overlaid with this non-instrumental character, taking us somewhere we don't really need to go and returning us to the very place we started. We're kicking a stone down the street and back again, to the glory of God.

Soon enough a child begins to play with a purpose—building with blocks, sculpting with sand, drawing with crayons, feeding the doll, keeping house, driving a truck, or riding the bus, whose wheels go round and round all through the town. Before long they realize they've entered unawares the actual world of work. They're singing the alphabet *(A, B, C, D, E, F, G . . .)*, frolicking through custodial chores *(Clean up! Clean up! Everybody, everywhere . . .)*, dolling up grammatical principles *(i before e except after c)*, and rhyming history *(in fourteen hundred and ninety-two, Columbus sailed the ocean blue)*. Is it a conspiracy, grown-ups luring the unwitting little critters under the guise of play for future conscription in the salt mines of society? No— it's simply our way of granting, particularly to tedious work, more suppleness than it might otherwise possess. No one with a thumb needs reminding that "nailing a nail" is not all fun and games, nor is picking peppers a walk in the park for those endowed with only a mortal's back. The singing, the rhyming, the counting, the timing—all of these possess the power to leaven the work to a certain lightness, and hi-ho, hi-ho, it's off to work we go.

If children are to be seen as prototypes for the why and wherefore of play, then play seems to be something of a doorway through which we pass on the way to larger life. Play punches the ticket for entry into that other world of greater responsibility that "real work" involves. That movement from one realm to the other persists through adulthood. When adults play, Diane Ackerman suggests we place ourselves in some "ordeal" or another—a task, a challenge, a predicament. For a biker, it may be completing a ride before the gathering storm moves in; for the runner, pushing for a little more distance than the last run or a slightly swifter pace; for the chess player, a strategic move under pressure. Ordeal, in the context of play, is managed and maneuverable—in other words, relatively safe. Successful deliverance from that ordeal has a way of equipping us for other more stringent life situations. If I can make it down a dicey run on the ski slopes, then when I'm off the mountain and back in street clothes I can more confidently negotiate other things as well—a complex work project, a difficult relationship, a tough personal discipline, a challenging situation at church or school or home.

Play has waltzed many a pizza chef through their shift, many a writer through their manuscript, many a hostage through their confinement. In *The Inextinguishable Symphony*, Martin Goldsmith relates the story of an Auschwitz survivor who was hours from extermination when it was discovered he had been a musician in a Berlin orchestra. He was spared the gas chamber and given the job of playing the cymbals at the neighboring camp of Birkenau. As prisoners left the camp for work in the morning and returned in the evening, he and a paltry group of prisoner-players would march them on their way. He soon became a favorite with the guards, who occasionally entertained themselves by throwing pebbles at him, which he fielded with his cymbals to generate a loud crash. By engaging in the child's play of his death-dealing captors, this man lived to tell about it.

If play can function as leverage for navigating difficult life experiences, it can also be a celebration of the blooming of the rose, the summiting of the mountain, the crowning of life. When Miriam danced in the light of the Exodus miracle (Exodus 15), she was celebrating with the Israelites the utter goodness of God. She and the people surely worked up a sweat with all their carrying on, but for the first time in four hundred years the sweating was by choice. The blending of work and play in that moment of creative dance had all the appearance of worship, a holy offering of praise and triumph. This is what Tom Driver surely meant—ritual is work done playfully. When we worship, we are working, creating, resting, and certainly playing—every last thing we were created to do and be, and, on a good day, we do so with a certain lightness of being, as though doxology were simply another word for breathing.

In worship or beyond, play is our way of saying yes to God, yes to life, yes to the pledge that whatever we meet next of marvel or surprise, we will meet it in trust, our dancing shoes ready. Truth be told, they're the same shoes that once took us to the work site as slaves and brought us home again as specters, the same shoes that one day carried us like the wind away from that God-awful place, the same shoes that sloshed through the mud to the free side of a forbidding sea. In such a pair of all-purpose shoes, these things begin to come together—the work and the play, the worship and the Sabbath, the rhyme and the reason, the *Pablito* and the *clavito*. With Yeats, we're left to wonder, "How can we know the dancer from the dance?"

part four

The Good Society

You are not primarily called to do, or to be;
you are called to belong.

E. Stanley Jones

Chapter 17

A Good Word for
Navel-gazing

I am because we are.
Catherine Kapikian

*I*n a sense, the most logical point of departure for a sense of creatureliness is the human navel, the most front-and-center piece of anatomical evidence that the human being is not self-invented. To look at ourselves closely, navel-gazing we sometimes call it, is to begin to realize that not only are our bodies hand-me-downs, but so is the very ability we possess even to consider them in the first place, identify their original source and purpose, and make relational connections accordingly. When on a lark you or I embark on a quest to find ourselves, whatever else we discover when we arrive, we are sure to meet a crowd.

From the Bantu tribe of South Africa comes the proverb, *Umuntu ungamuntu ungabantu.* For those who are not up to speed on their Bantu, this translates to mean, "A person is a person through other persons." The saying stands in contrast to certain Western philosophies of identity, typified by the classic Descartes formula from the seventeenth century, *Cogito ergo sum,* "I think, therefore I am." By this logic, what defines me irrefutably as an entity, a person, an *individual*, is my ability to function cognitively. The Bantu sense of life is something more along these lines: What defines me as a person is my connection with others, my claim upon them and theirs upon me, and the myriad ways that life comes to expression and fulfillment in this endless reciprocal matrix. I am related, therefore I am.

Some years ago, country music artist Jessica Andrews gave voice to this view of life with a song that spoke to that matrix of relationships and its power, beyond any particular talent or achievement, to establish and fortify our sense of "who I am":

> *I am Rosemary's granddaughter*
> *The spitting image of my father.*

Singing through the rest of the song's lyrics, you'll notice that, in terms of pronoun count, the "I's" have it—the singer speaks of herself early and often. There's nothing terribly unusual about that—with a very few exceptions, we tend to be our own favorite subject. (Twelve-step groups have a saying: "I'm not much, but I'm all I think about.") However, the ways in which the singer makes positive reference to herself are relational and derivative rather than intrinsic or autonomous. They involve other people rather than being based solely upon "who I am" or "what I've done." Rosemary's granddaughter, who looks just like her father and knows her mother's affirmation and her friends' enveloping, has clearly spent some time navel-gazing—in the best sense of the term. She seems to have discovered what is true for all of us: she is nothing if not connected.

The myth that we are self-made creatures, which has been discussed earlier, becomes untenable the moment we realize that others have both created and now sustain my very existence. To extend the reality further, "others" means more than simply Dad, Mom, and Grandmother Rosemary. The circle of sustenance continues far beyond those I know and love, who know and love me in return.

Arguably, people we will never know are more responsible for our well-being than those who gave us birth or offer us enduring friendship. Think about it for a moment. Do you know who oversees the purification of your drinking water? Who tested the tires on your car? Who grew the wheat for the bread on your sandwich? Who taught the faith to your parents? Who preserved the first parchment version of the Gospel of Mark? Do you know the name of the doctor or midwife who delivered you from the womb or the instructor who taught them their methods? Surely you know the name of the person who engineered the highway overpass over which you recently drove; after all, you put your life in their hands the moment you started up the ramp. Without these people, most of whose names we will never know, we might be dead, hungry, or too sick to care. Since we do not have the benefit of knowing their names, we've grown accustomed to calling them something else: perfect strangers.

If we paused to consider even the ways we can *think* of in which these perfect strangers contribute minute by minute to our safety and well-being, our sense of beholdenness would likely overwhelm us. As with a symbiotic relationship in nature—bees and flowers, for example—we are reliant for our very existence on this intricate matrix of goods and services; those who offer them so routinely and unassumingly are in turn reliant on countless others, including us, for theirs. How can we possibly say thanks?

Obrigado is how the Brazilians say it. Portuguese for *thank you*, it means, literally, "obligated." And so we are. My existence and identity are daily borrowed from a social, psychological, spiritual, and biological bank to which I owe an ever-mounting debt. The only accepted currency of repayment I know is becoming myself a perfect stranger for others, giving myself over to these connections that have meant life to me.

The moment we recognize that others' long and winding roads to finding themselves lead to our door, we become responsible. No longer can I see my life as my own. Everything I am and do is witnessed, and woven into the warp and woof of others' character and calling. "I can never be what I ought to be until you are what you ought to be," Martin Luther King, Jr. once observed. "And you can never be what you ought to be until I am what I ought to be." We're in this together, not by choice, but by birthright.

Creatureliness as an outlook on life takes its cue from this awareness that we are all hand-me-downs, connected to others as part of our very constitution. What we see when we gaze at our navel is that life preceded us, gave us our birth, tied the knot, and cut the cord. The very existence of any life is predicated upon the existence of others' lives. I am related, therefore I am.

Think of the knot that tied off your umbilical cord as a permanent reminder—a piece of string tied to your core instead of around your finger. Let it serve to remind you that you are beholden to an entire planet of people, places, and things, beginning with the perfect stranger behind the blue-green mask who did you the lifelong courtesy of placing the reminder there in the first place. With every respiration, the ribbon extends outward to the world and back in to your own center, out to receive, in to make use of what has been received; then out to give what has been generated within, and in for further mining. In such a way might we come to know that the question of who we are, although having many complex answers, has one that is blessedly simple. Who am I? Yours.

Chapter 18

Retying the Lace

Blest be the tie that binds . . .
John Fawcett

Something there is that wants a shoelace tied, that causes us to zero in on a flopping shoestring the way a cheetah tracks its prey. Is it safety? Tripping over your own untied shoelace is a universal hazard, isn't it? From the time we're able to put on lace-up shoes, or even have them put on for us, we run the risk of one untied shoestring getting stepped on by the other foot and sending us reeling.

I carry scars on the four fingers of my left hand from a day ten years ago when I performed that very dance sequence: right shoestring works itself loose and begins flailing in the air, left shoe plants itself squarely on top of it, right foot is caught up short, body reels—all the way to Virginia. What's more, at the time I was running behind a baby jogger that held our youngest child, Anna. When I lurched forward after tripping on the string, instinct had me holding firmly to the crossbar of the jogger, which meant not having a second hand free to brace my fall. When all was said and done, I was sprawled out on the pavement. My left hand, still gripping the handle, was pressed against the asphalt, four knuckles scraped fairly raw. As for Anna, she was lying, pretty as you please, flat on her back in the upturned stroller, quietly gazing at the clear blue sky.

Safety is surely part of that something that wants a shoelace tied. But there's more. Is it aesthetics? Goodness knows a long shoestring flopping around is about as pleasing to the eye as a window shutter dangling from its hinge. When I was in elementary school the word on the street was that our principal carried a pair of scissors in his suit pocket for cutting off shirttails and shoelaces that weren't in their proper places, tucked in and tied, respectively. This urban legend, true or not, wasn't about safety—it was a matter of decorum: tails belong tucked and laces belong tied.

Even so, besides safety and presentability, there's something else altogether that wants a shoelace tied. When we notice an untied shoe and have an urge to see it tied, I want to say it's a kind of completeness we're after—to see a thing arrive at what it's meant to be. When you think of it, that process of completion is how our entire lives are lived out and hoped along. We wait for conception to be completed in birth, for a child to grow into maturity as an adult, for ourselves to grow over a lifetime toward "perfection in love," as John Wesley would say it. I've shared the work on a Habitat for Humanity house toward the day when a family would stand on the freshly painted front porch and accept the keys while someone's handkerchief accepted the tears. That's completion.

The completion of our prayers is the *Amen*, the "so-be-it," when all that's been sung or shouted, whispered or sighed is let go of and entrusted to God. There's the completion of a death. We walk that ragged meadow of letting go, the last farewell, the calls and casseroles, the "sweeping up the heart and putting love away," and finally must seal the earth or urn over our loved one's remains, and turn to walk now a different direction, toward the vacancy of home. The completion of a grief is others to love. The completion of a long journey is arriving back at our own doorstep, where we wipe our weary feet and step inside to the familiar, changed.

Religion is that yearning deep within us to move toward completion in all of life's dimensions—to see lives fulfilled and the world made whole. The word "religion" is itself the completing of two half-words that were practically made for each other. *Re* we recognize as meaning "again," as in *re*peat, *re*visit, *re*new, and even *re*cognize. *Ligion* is a little less transparent, but still fairly simple to identify. We see it in *liaison, ligament,* and *ligature,* and it means "connection" or, to pick up a strand we've already been following, "tie together." Tie together *re* and *ligion,* and you have *religion,* "tying together again."

Religion begins with the realization that we are at loose ends in our relationship with God, others, the created order, even ourselves. Rudolph Bultmann once wrote that we carry within us a faint recollection of the garden of Eden. I would suppose that includes a vague and sinking memory of that "Adam, where are you?" conversation with God as well as the delightfully sublime communion that preceded it. From that innate recollection we are persuaded both that the world is incomplete and that it might be otherwise. We then seek means to reconcile that which is estranged, bind up that which is unbound, "retie" that unraveled string of relationships. It may begin with shoestrings, but soon moves to those who wear them, and then to those who have none to wear in the first place, and then the common earth they both tread, and finally the one God to whom all their wandering leads.

The primary ways in which we relate to God and seek to see the world complete through a life with God are prayer and self-giving. In the act of praying, we often clasp our hands together, fingers braided like a shoelace tied, or friends rejoined, or lovers reunited. Sometimes the braiding is hands around a circle of prayer or the community gathered in for worship. Whatever expression prayer takes, it forms a loom we might call surrender, and the weaving work begins. Lament is woven into praise, past meets future, confession pardon, memory hope. Reality and dream are joined, as are doubt and faith, enemy and friend, sister and brother, forgiver and forgiven, individual and world. Think of those clasped hands, or those hands joined with others, the left finding its way to the right, the right to the left, as the way we seek to hold up the stray and stuttering facets of our lives, our world, our relationship with God, trusting God to bind them into a mended whole, into completeness. Remember the Lord's Prayer: *Hallowed* be your name, *whole and uninjured*. The more earnest the prayer, the tighter the clasping—a double-knotting of the shoelace against its coming untied.

Once we turn our hopes toward God for help in pulling together disparate things, holding lightly to unfinished things, brokering some complicated peace among dissonant things, we discover something besides the fact that God possesses string long enough for the task. We discover the string has been long since wending its way into place, already working long before we knew of it to bind and bless our lives and world into *shalom*. In fact, that very string has drawn us to God in the first place, and to the world. "You knit me together in my mother's womb," the psalmist says of God (Psalm 139:13). In the rebinding work of religion, we are both early beneficiaries and lifetime benefactors.

Leading from our prayers and turning us again to prayer, self-giving is the other dimension of our life with God, part and parcel of the first. We aim to see the world reconciled, the cup of water offered to the thirsty, the lost found, the wounded whole, the good news shared and lived. By love's strong cord we find that God uses us to pull down the walls of injustice and set the captive free. Others desire healing for a loved one or deliverance from a grief or illness. We learn that life and wholeness are rather delicate mysteries, held in the durable web of

God's mercy and grace. Or we long to satisfy somehow, somewhere the thirsting of our own souls for something more than the usual something more. We have sought a hundred other means for quenching that thirst, but in vain, for some invisible tether persists in pulling us back to our place of honest need. When through tears and running laughter we finally discover that with God is the fountain of life, our cup overflows.

True religion ties us to God and others in ways that are both supple and inextricable. Its practices of prayer and self-giving lead us upward, inward, and outward with all the shared affections of our faith—modesty, trust, longing, faith, compassion, hopefulness, lament, joy. Once I have begun to experience and live into these affections, I will less and less be able to think of myself in isolation. And less and less will I wish to do so, for the same ties that bind me to others in their need bind them also to me in mine. What we learn anatomically from reflection on our own navel is confirmed spiritually, as through the interlaced practices of prayer and self-giving religion takes hold: we are of a piece.

Chapter 19

The Mean of Grace

Community wounds even as it blesses.
Thomas E. Clarke, SJ

*H*ow many people do you know who've given up on organized religion? Perhaps you're one of them. For these people, institutional religion is regarded as a spent formula,
out-of-date and out-of-touch. The very word *religion*, even
without any of its cumbersome qualifiers, is suspect to some.
The Museum of Modern Art in Fort Worth recently featured
"an exhibit not about religion, but our persistent reach for
heaven." I'm still trying to figure out the difference between
the two. I've heard one concern, often attributed to Carl Jung,
voiced more times than I can count: "A great deal of institutional religion seems designed to prevent the faithful from having a spiritual experience." For many, "religion" has become a
convenient castoff, right up there with Styrofoam and water
bottles. In its place, we've found something that promises all
the same benefits without so many of the bothersome features:
private spirituality.

Personally, I have nothing against private spirituality, except
when it claims to be in any way related to Christianity.
Christian faith is incubated and forged in the company of others. Where there is no community, there is no Christianity.

Even hermits in isolation deliberately and methodically—we could even say religiously—draw their sustenance for the life of prayer and solitude from the Christian community. For the follower of Jesus, faith is born and nurtured in the footsteps created by other followers along the same path. Bishop William Willimon has put it this way: "Christianity is not spiritual; it's incarnational." In other words, Christian faith is not about my own private delights and discoveries; it is about my neighbor's bread and drink.

Speaking of bread and drink, the church's two sacraments, baptism and the Lord's Supper, draw us into the community's life and faith with a tenacity to beat the band. In their very essence they are fiercely unprivatizable, though I'm not so sure that can't be said of virtually everything in life. The font and table are inherently plural both in their meanings and their applications.

We have come to call these two sacraments "means of grace," meaning that through the sign-acts of water, bread, and cup we understand grace to be conveyed. Think of them as channels, or vessels, of God's forgiving, renewing, empowering love. In my mind, these means of grace also function as the *mean* of grace, that is, the centering function of grace. They carry out that aspect of grace that has to do with ignoring us in just the right measure for the sake of drawing us into the community's ongoing common life. Whether we like it or not, font and table are spread in the motley company of "organized religion." In the course of time we will be bathing, wining, and dining with princess-complexed Sister Saturnalia and bombastic Brother Behemoth. When we decide we're too good for these two, thank you very much, then we're too big for our own britches besides, and font and table bring us back down to size, no private parties at this poolside restaurant. Likewise, when our tune is "Woe is me—I am unworthy of the church and don't belong," neither font nor table pay us any mind, but continue to expect our attendance. "The things that ignore us," observes Andrew Harvey, "save us in the end." Beginning, perhaps, with what happens through the mean of grace in water, bread, and wine.

Baptism, like the marriage vow, is impossible to undertake alone. In a service of marriage, we are wed into a covenant relationship, and so with the font of baptism. Instead of bride or groom, think of baptized and congregation. Will you have this community of faith? "I will." Community, will you have this newly baptized one? "We will." Will you both have God, who already has you? "We will." Vows, rings, holy kiss. Those whom God has joined together, let no one put asunder.

Now begins the fun. The joy of teaching the stories and songs of the faith to the newly baptized; the wonder of witnessing the virtues of adequacy, generosity, and trust practiced across aisles, across age groups, across years; the strains of sharing the work in close quarters, bumping into each other on occasion, or often; the beauty of voices joined in worship—my agreeing to sing the song I know you pin your hopes on and your willingness to sing a song that helps keep me alive in the faith; tensions over how to be the church—green carpet or red? This mission or that? Spend or save? Raise a roof or feed the poor? There is deep gratitude when I am thirsty and you give me to drink, and deep hurt—even disillusionment—when I am sick, and the preoccupied church visits me not. If all goes according to plan, even in those rending moments, grace appears. For church is nothing if not a school of forgiveness.

The thing that's good and bad about private spirituality is there's no one around to make forgiveness a requirement. It's mostly bad, of course. Who wants to be always right, given the price—perpetual estrangement from those who know and love you? *Live alone in a paradise that makes me think of two.*

This may sound strange in one way, and extremely obvious in another, but Holy Communion is principally about hospitality.

Certainly we see the hospitality of God in the words of Jesus at the table in the Upper Room, "This is my body, given for you . . ." This gesture is the fundamental touchstone of divine grace—Jesus self-giving for the life of the world. Interesting that the hospitality of the disciples led the way to that sacred moment, Jesus having sent them ahead to prepare the place. In the Emmaus story, what we sometimes call "the first supper" following the resurrection, two disciples invited the stranger with whom they traveled into their home, and to their table, furnishing bread and cup for the meal. Again, their hospitality led the way for that of the stranger, who accepted their gift of bread, blessed it, broke it, and shared it with them. In the breaking of the bread, their eyes were opened, and they recognized the stranger as the risen Christ (Luke 24:13-35).

In the open meadow, with thousands on hand hungering for the gospel, but eventually for other sorts of food as well, Jesus turned to his disciples and said, "You give them something to eat." They drew from the hospitality of the crowd. Again, Jesus accepted their gift, then turned the moment sacramental: he took the bread, blessed and broke it, and gave it to the disciples to feed the multitudes (Mark 6:30-44). So far, the Lord's Supper is all about finding accommodations, making provision, offering a loaf, a cup, a life—not just on the part of Jesus the host, but by all who bring to the feast whatever they have and are.

For the apostle Paul, the table practices of the early church center on this one matter of hospitality. Some are inconsiderately going ahead with the holy meal before others have even arrived for the service. In addressing this behavior, Paul takes a roundabout path, but by the end of the discussion he essentially has one thing to tell them, the same thing you and I learned at manners school: wait for one another. With a single stroke of the quill, he has arrived at the heart of the matter, the centering word, the mean of grace: others (1 Corinthians 11).

When Paul says "discern the body of Christ," he doesn't expect this can be done in isolation, for God is best seen with the collective eyes of community. What we do at table, and at the font, *we* do at the table and font, *together*. Why? Precisely because *together* is the only way the water, bread, and wine can be perceived and shared in ways that mean grace.

When we speak of these elements as *channels* of grace, then by extension we who take them upon and within ourselves become channels of grace as well. Our nourishment is not the final destination for the grace of the sacrament. We are filled to be emptied for one another, washed to be worn, perhaps even tattered and torn, by the serving work. We are saved, someone has said, not for ourselves, but for the joy of others. And as we offer that joy, our own is completed. "Pour us full," my colleague prays, as though we were a pitcher brimmed for pouring another's wine, made ready for the welcome table by the means and mean of grace.

Chapter 20

Greatness in a Shrub

All God's critters got a place in the choir—
Some sing low, some sing higher . . .
Bill Staines

*I*f "religion" is about tying things together—ourselves to each other and creation, and all of us to God, then what does that suggest about our relationship to the world outside the circle of the church? Are God's people Biosphere II, with a bubble over everything Christian, and all food, supplies, and sunlight stored under a dome topped with a neatly tied bow? Obviously not—the world needs us, and we need the world. Besides, how could we ever store that many chicken casseroles under one roof? Our lives in Christian community require connection to the world.

Even so, there are certainly steps we could take to pull away from the societal influences we find objectionable. We can home-school our children, live in gated communities, participate only in church-related extracurricular activities, work only for a "Christian" boss, and so on. There are many ways we can remove ourselves from the secular mainstream. But should we?

If we were to isolate ourselves from society, then how would people like you and me ever have found our way into the church in the first place? Somebody somewhere crossed the boundary between church and world to bring good news to you, or to your parents, or to theirs. And what about those yet to hear good news in a language they can understand—who will bear that gift to them? Gating the church community is clearly not a Christian option. So how does the church relate to the world in winning ways?

There are at least two "great commissions" in the Gospel of Matthew, one that says "Come," the other that says, "Go." "Come to me, all you that are weary" (Matthew 11:28). "Go and disciple all nations" (Matthew 28:19, paraphrase). In this chapter and the next I will explore the "come and go" dynamic between the church and the world as ingredient to the good society.

In the context of the Gospels, Jesus' words inviting to himself all who are weary almost seem redundant. People are already flocking to him from city and countryside, seeking to discover his healing presence, his powerful teaching, his claim upon their lives. The commission to "come to me . . ." hardly needs commanding, which makes me wonder if that particular "great commission" isn't meant to be *overheard* as much as heard. This probably isn't true at your church or mine, but church members may sometimes need reminding that the church exists for the world rather than for itself, which means doors are open and welcome given not only to the pedigreed, the polished, and the proven, but to the least, the last, and the lost. *All* who are weary, come. If you happen at the moment to be among the weary, congratulations—this is your lucky day! If you don't, pay close attention here.

Just fluttering distance from this commissioning verse in Matthew is a parable about the look and feel of God's new society, which is sometimes called "the kingdom of heaven." This story, as so many of Jesus' parables, is also about the look and feel of the church as it tries to reflect and embody that new society in the way it lives. The parable, found in Matthew 13:31-32, is brief enough to retell here:

The kingdom of heaven is like a mustard seed that someone took and sowed in his field; it is the smallest of all the seeds, but when it has grown it is the greatest of shrubs and becomes a tree, so that the birds of the air come and make nests in its branches.

If I were to cover those verses for a moment with a bookmark and ask you to tell me about the mustard seed parable, you'd probably say it was a story about faith. I used to think so too; then I realized that's the *other* mustard seed saying—about faith to move mountains or mulberry trees—and it appears elsewhere (Matthew 17 and Luke 17, respectively).

This parable is not ostensibly about faith like those other two, but about something very small ("the smallest of seeds") growing into something very big ("the greatest of shrubs"), which is in some ways very much about faith after all. At any rate, greatness in itself is an appealing subject, even for the church. The disciples wanted to be great, and we wouldn't want to rule out the possibility for ourselves, either. Don't you want your church to be great—prominent, well-respected in the community, striking a handsome presence, growing in numbers, prospering financially? And the church in society and around the world—don't we want its presence and influence to be great?

Jesus' parable clearly has another vision for his followers, and for the kingdom they represent in their life together. His idea of "greatness" is, well, a shrub. Tell me, when is the last time you heard the words "great" and "shrub" in the same sentence? Well, now it's happened twice in a single paragraph. Consider this fair warning.

Metaphors for prominent kingdoms were common in biblical times. In Daniel 4, King Nebuchadnezzar is identified as a great tree, strong and beautiful, towering above the forest, providing food and shelter for all, the epitome of nobility, power, and benevolence. In Ezekiel 31, Assyria is likened to a cedar of Lebanon, tall and fair, with "all the birds of the air" making nests in its branches. Sound familiar? Elsewhere in Ezekiel, the prophet envisions Israel being planted as a sprig on a "high and lofty mountain," growing up to become "a noble cedar," under which "every kind of bird will live." Psalm 92:12 declares that "the righteous flourish like the palm tree, and grow like a cedar in Lebanon."

Seeing a pattern here? Massive trees equal greatness. It made for a very useful metaphor then; it does yet. Enter Jesus, who, pondering the best metaphor to characterize God's kingdom, comes up with . . . a *shrub*. Imagine the look on his listeners' faces! Better yet, go look in a mirror, and you won't have to imagine anything. After Israel's long, proud tradition of aspiring to the highest reaches of the atmosphere, commanding respect, dominating the landscape, Jesus essentially subverts the metaphor, swapping out the tall, stately tree for a big, gangly bush. One element is carried forward—it seems to be the only one Jesus believes is worth retaining: birds of the air still have refuge in the branches of the shrub. In fact, that facet becomes the centerpiece of the image—nothing else about this great big shrub is noteworthy but the fact that there are birds in its branches, availing themselves of the free rent.

You and I know about birds. By and large, we love them—as long as they don't build their nests under our porch. They sing lovely songs, but also carry disease. They inspire poets with their flights of fancy but also function as top-flight bombardiers with special skill in identifying newly washed cars.

I can watch birds for hours as they forage for worms, bugs, or seeds. But during the time I'm *not*, they will devour my corn crop and think nothing of it. And they are not always courtly toward each other, either. Sparrows are the bane of bluebirds' existence. Jays can bully little wrens like the devil.

All of these birds—the good, the bad, and the ugly—are finding nests in the branches of the great mustard shrub. Did I say *great*? Frumpy, gangly, ungraceful, unwieldy—these might be better adjectives to put in front of this mustard shrub, now overrun with birds, filled with their chatter, covered in their droppings. Did I say *great*? No, Jesus did.

Taking our lead from the parable, the church, then, becomes to the world as a mustard shrub, into whose branches all the birds of the air may come to nest. Its greatness is not in handsomeness, stature, or dominance, but in accommodation and hospitality—how many birds it can fit beneath its boughs, and how well. Some picture of the church, huh? Take a good, hard look. That, Jesus said, is your future.

Are we ready to open the doors of the church to just anyone—the rude, the raucous, the unschooled, the unmannered? I'm not sure. And then I think of myself on my worst days—maybe on any given day—and I remember that sometime somewhere someone opened the doors for me, saw fit to take me in, train me, teach me, forgive me, call me, send me, bless me. There are days when I am sure that *I* am one of those birds, and not an operatic thrush or stunning redwing, more likely a sparrow, a crow, or a pigeon. And still I belong.

We can all relate. In terms of our smooth versus shrill vocalizations, none of us are perfect-pitch nightingales. I hope you and I are progressing nicely in that direction, but, let's be honest, God is not through with us yet.

How does the church relate to the world? By opening its doors, its ministries, its heart to "all who are weary." By becoming a beacon of grace and acceptance to whoever seeks shelter and shade from life's storms, with a threshold for inclusion as low as the lowest branch of a mustard shrub. By embracing all sorts of "birds" rather than a specific variety, and drawing its pride not from being a showpiece but from being a busy, loud, messy, beautiful nesting ground for any and for all.

How does the church relate to the world? In a way, we might see Jesus as our model—not just his paradoxical parable about shrubby greatness, but *him*. On the cross in his suffering, before the cross in his ministry, and after the cross as the risen Christ, he spreads his arms wide toward the world much like the branches of a tree, offering compassion, forgiveness, salvation, life. Come to me, *all*.

Next time you're sizing up churches, yours or any other, or even Christianity in general, don't ask how high its branches reach, but how wide; not, is its form stately and handsome, but is it short and squat and gangly enough so as to provide the best shade and shelter for nesters and their young. Don't ask how dashing a figure its building cuts against the landscape, but what are its figures on welcoming people—people desirable by society's standard, and otherwise. It's far from the sort of greatness we're used to hearing about, certainly from the world— and even sometimes in the churches. Personally, I would call it modest, except that Jesus has already called it great. Maybe in the ways of the kingdom they're one and the same.

> *When Christ was raised from death to life*
> *the cross became a tree,*
> *and there beneath its mending branch*
> *raised up to life are we.*

Chapter 21

The Whole World Home

The gospel of Christ knows no religion but social;
no holiness but social holiness.
John Wesley

*W*hen Jesus prayed for God's rule of justice and mercy to come into the world, he didn't pray, "Let your kingdom come, your will be done *in the church* as in heaven." His words were rather "Let your kingdom come, your will be done *on earth* as in heaven." "Earth's the right place for love," wrote Robert Frost. Jesus seemed to think so too. His very last words to his followers at the end of Matthew, what I have called the second great commission of that Gospel, are all about the *on earth* part of that prayer: "Go, therefore, and disciple all nations . . ."

The commandment leaves no uncertainty as to what is called for—the same as what was asked of Abram and Sarai, of Moses, of Jonah, Jeremiah, Mary, and Paul. Unsettle yourself from where you are now, bring the goodness of your experience of God with you, and offer it to a world yearning for goodness and for God. Bring also the brightness of your light, and offer it to a world feeling its way in the dark.

If we were to identify in Matthew's Gospel similar teachings and charges along the way to this culminating commissioning moment, we would find various places from which these final words of Jesus picked up their currency. One of them would certainly be Matthew 5:14-16, where Jesus makes a startling announcement to his listeners: "You are the light of the world." *We?* The light of the world? If he had said, "*I* am the light of the world," which is a claim made a few Gospels to the right, we would go with that willingly. But *we* as the *church* are the light of the world?

When God called Abram and Sarai from their cozy suburban home in Haran, he said "I will bless you, and make your name great, so that you will be a blessing" (Genesis 12:2). One ancient commentary on this text speaks of that encounter this way: "Why did Abraham have to go forth to the world? At home, he was like a flask of myrrh with a tight-fitting lid. Only when it is open can the fragrance be scattered to the winds."

The church's mission is to spill out of the flask and into the world, carrying a fragrance that touches, heals, converts, and blesses, turning the hearts of children to their parents, as the prophet put it, and of the parents to their young, and the hearts of all to God. Jesus goes on with his words about us being light: "let your light shine before others, so that they may see your good works and give glory to your Father in heaven" (Matthew 5:16). The rekindling, retying, reconciling, hope-giving, fragrance-carrying, light-bringing work of religion is for the sanctuary, to be sure, but it is also for the marketplace, and far beyond.

The autumn of 1989 witnessed one of the most breathtaking socio-political events in modern history, what we've come to refer to, broadly speaking, as the Velvet Revolution. Practically overnight Communist regimes in the Soviet bloc were toppling, yet with a minimum of bloodshed. The domino theory of the Cold War era was finally being proved, only in reverse. Every government collapse in the Eastern European region seemed to lead to another. Some called it a magical moment, others a miracle; perhaps it was some of both.

What often went unseen during that process were some of the underpinnings of that transfer of power, including the church's role in cultivating the movement for cultural and political freedom. One example comes from Leipzig, East Germany, where during public demonstrations early in the fall of 1989 a banner could be seen hanging over the crowd. It read, "Wir danken dir Kirche." *We thank you, Church*. It was a reference to Nicholai Church, a cathedral church in the heart of Leipzig, dog-eared and dilapidated after decades of government opposition and antagonism.

Years earlier a small group within the remnant congregation began to gather on Monday evenings to pray for peace and freedom in their nation. Monday after Monday, week after week, year after year, that group came together to pray. In May 1989 the larger community began to take greater notice, and gradually the small group began to grow.

By summer the state police had begun to monitor these prayer services—they were no longer small enough to stay beneath the radar of state surveillance and obstruction. On September 4, as the group was leaving the church, they were attacked by the police. At that point, they could have either fought back or cancelled the prayer meetings. They did neither. Instead, they went to the Gospels for guidance and carried on with their meetings, having decided, should they be attacked again, to use nonviolence as a response.

The group continued to grow, exponentially now, and on September 25, six thousand people packed the cathedral for the Monday night prayer service. The following Monday, October 2, twenty thousand peaceful protesters waited outside the doors of the cathedral. Within days, the East German world had been overturned as gently as an omelet.

The late German theologian Karl Barth, who witnessed in the 1930s the rise of the Third Reich and subsequent appropriation of East Germany by Soviet Russia as a communist satellite, did not live to see the day of his divided country's liberation. But in that historic moment in 1989 when the Jericho walls came down not with a battle but with a prayer, his words from half a century earlier proved prophetic: to clasp the hands in prayer is the beginning of an uprising against the disorder of this world.

Salt, light, fragrance—the transformation of society through immersion in its life and systems in courageous and life-giving ways—it is the power of a violet breaking through the rocks. It is a lamp quietly burning, gently raised, giving light to all, and warmth besides.

In his novel, *Son of Laughter,* Frederick Buechner has Jacob musing about the meaning of that strange blessing given to his grandfather long ago, the one we spoke of above: "I will bless you, and make your name great, *so that* you will be a blessing" (Genesis 12:2, emphasis mine). The awareness that the gift of a blessing is not to be kept, but shared, is dawning on him and leads him to the same illuminating metaphor that has flooded our chapter:

> *[God] is always shielding us like a guttering wick . . . because the fire he is trying to start with us is a fire that the whole world will live to warm its hands at. It is a fire in the dark that will light the whole world home.*

part
five

The Good Earth

Every blade of grass has its
Angel that bends over
it and whispers, "Grow, grow."

The Talmud

Chapter 22

Earth's Possession

Why, then the world's mine oyster,
Which I with sword will open.
William Shakespeare

The one who is of the earth belongs to the earth . . .
The words of Jesus, John 3:31

"The land was ours before we were the land's." So began the poem recited by Robert Frost at the inauguration of John F. Kennedy as the thirty-fifth president of the United States of America. The year was 1961, the bookend to an era we've come to call the Baby Boom for the number of post–World War II births it produced. But the boom involved more than babies— a general sense of fecundity and enterprise pervaded the national mind-set through those post-war years. America saw opportunity on every corner and possibility over every horizon. It was a new frontier movement, and as with those that preceded it, this movement made grand assumptions regarding the continent and its possession. The land was ours.

Half a century later, we are in a considerably more reflective state concerning our world, and certainly our environment. We are akin to the boy who dreamed he ate a giant marshmallow and awoke to find his pillow missing. Certain aspects of our American dream have involved such sizable appetites, and there is a sense in which we have satisfied them virtually in our sleep. But what are we to do about our missing pillow? We are just now beginning to awaken to such questions regarding the implications of our lifestyles on the environment we inhabit and lay our heads upon.

In the process, we have discovered a new conversation partner—earth. Suddenly, our planet is talking back to us, something to which we're thoroughly unaccustomed. The language it speaks is distinct but perfectly intelligible; after all, it is our mother tongue. The heavens are telling the glory of God, and the earth declares humanity's handiwork: melting glaciers, polluted rivers, thinning ozone, shrinking rain forests, depleted aquifers, and disappearing species. "No, the land was not yours before you were the land's. You are, and always have been, earth's possession. You've enjoyed a hundred-year joyride in a borrowed car, but you've just run out of gas, blown a tire, and come upon a tree fallen across the road. The ride is over. Now come on home."

Our history lessons have long presented the Tigris-Euphrates River basin as the "cradle of civilization," suggesting that human civilization owes its very existence to a place, a land area, a geography. Genesis recounts that we were drawn up *from the dust of the earth* and given the breath of life. God specifically charged Adam and Eve with the guardianship and protection of this earth from which they came: your job is to love your mother, to cultivate this marvelous cradle of a garden from which you have lately sprung. It was to have been a modest but deeply satisfying role. They said no; they wanted more. And less has been their lot ever since, and ours.

It is time we quieted ourselves to listen for the inner ache that comes from somewhere deeper than our growling stomachs. It is an ache similar to that of a child suddenly lost from mom and dad at the amusement park. Worthy parental-unit substitutes are everywhere to be seen, but somehow that doesn't assuage the dread. I once saw a mallard duck pacing anxiously in the median of a boulevard. I thought its behavior was odd until my eyes turned to the far lane of the busy street, where its severely injured partner lay in an irretrievable heap on the road. The mallard's is the ache of which I speak.

It is the ache of Samuel Taylor Coleridge's ancient mariner, whose desolate ship was stranded on the southern ice floes, leaving him and his crew trapped and desperate. An albatross appeared, and with it, freedom. The winds blew northward, the ice parted, and the craft was at sail again. The mariner and crew were saved from certain death. God be praised! The beautiful bird lingered auspiciously, befriending those whose lives it had spared. And then, tragedy struck. Actually, insanity is probably a better word. The mariner raised his crossbow, took aim at the blessed bird, and shot it. Why he did so he could not later explain, only that the ache of regret for his heinous and insensible deed haunted him to the end of his days.

For a million seasons the automatic earth has yielded its goodness, bounty upon bounty, harvest after harvest, crops, coal, oil, gold, timber, water, ore. We have partaken of these treasures, respectfully in some cases, ransackingly in many more. The earth has been patient with our plundering, ever giving, ever blessing, the sun and the rain and the apple seed. And then, for greed, or glory, or in the ignorance of a dreamer eating his or her pillow, we have raised the crossbow, taken aim, and let the arrow fly.

Coleridge was a prophet ahead of his time. When he published *The Rime of the Ancient Mariner,* it must have seemed rhapsodic to his readers, a maudlin allegory of spiritual maladies. How could he have known that, two centuries later, this generation's readers would recognize themselves in the story and see the poem not as melodramatic flair, but as national memoir. In the wake of the tragedy, the corpse of the albatross was draped by the crew around the mariner's neck, where he wore it thereafter. We have come to speak of "the albatross around our neck" to refer to a burden, an unwelcome obliga-tion, an unpleasant problem. Ours is indeed the burden of liv-ing in the awareness that the good earth has been felled like a great bird, or a towering oak, or a mother buffalo, her totter-ing calf left bawling across the desolate plain.

The earth has never been our possession, always our posses-sor. We may have relinquished guardianship for it, but it has never ceased to be guardian to us, a mother providing for our every need as best she can, often in spite of us. As is true with off-spring, we benefit from belonging more than we generally know.

The good news is that a mother possesses immortal powers of the sort that allow her to endure slings and arrows, and love the more—to a point. What is needed in our time is a wake-up call of biblical proportions to stem the tide of environmental destruc-tion. Can we harness the frontier enterprise of the Boom era for the purposes of crafting applications of technologies that better sustain us *and* our earth? Not "the land is ours," but "the creative challenge is ours." We know how to reduce smog in the cities, and have done so. We know how to reduce acid rain in the forests, and have done so. On the road today is a certain make of hybrid-powered automobile that is *faster* than its gasoline-powered coun-terpart and yet uses 40 percent less fuel. Ingenuity, when applied to worthwhile causes, can yield extraordinary results. What has begun ominously may yet become sorrow's springs.

Mother is calling us home from our imaginary escapades, our puffed-up feats of derring-do, our make-believe conquests of land, sea, and sky. Oh, mother, please, do you have to remind us that it's all pretend? She ignores us. "Leave your crossbows at the door and go wash up for supper." The hearth is warm, the feast is ample, but if we go in we'll have to put up with all those rules: No elbows on the table. Save some for others. Wait for the bless-ing. Then again, we've been a long time gone, and we're awfully hungry, though not for food so much as for a place at the table. Belonging, we're coming to learn, is a hunger all its own.

Chapter 23

Following Seasons

Do you not say, "Four months more,
then comes the harvest"?
The words of Jesus, John 4:35

So teach us to number our days that we
may get a heart of wisdom.
Psalm 90:12 (RSV)

*E*mily Dickinson once quipped that the only commandment
from the Bible she ever observed was "Consider the lilies of
the field . . ." (Matthew 6:28). Her remark calls to mind an
astonishing dimension of Jesus' life and teaching, one to which
we have historically given little attention: the way in which
nature and the seasons are woven into both his consciousness
and his gospel proclamation. "Look at the fig tree and all the
trees," he once told his listeners. "The wind blows where it
chooses, and you hear the sound of it . . ." "Lightning comes
from the east and flashes as far as the west . . ." "Where the
corpse is, there the vultures will gather . . ." "A sower went out
to sow . . ." "I sent you to reap that for which you did not labor."
"The earth produces of itself, we know not how . . ." "Consider
the birds of the air . . ." "Consider the lilies of the field."

Why was Jesus so keen on crops, so knowledgeable of nature—both its methods and its mystery? Was it because he was part of a rural farming culture, in which life was lived close to the earth? As a child, I would once in a blue moon be the lucky recipient of a letter from my maternal grandfather, typed hunt-and-peck on an old manual typewriter. I'm sure that machine was eligible even then for display at a museum, but Granddad still had plenty of use for it right there at his desk.

He and my grandmother were small-range ranchers and big-garden farmers. Their Angus cattle never topped a hundred head; at the same time, their vegetable garden was sizable—easily bigger than a basketball court. At any rate, Granddad's letters never failed to include mention of the weather, the seasons, the crops. It was dry—we needed rain. Or the hay was going to make pretty good this year. Pecans were showing in the trees by now—we should have a nice crop. The spring garden's coming along all right. I remember, even as a child, being aware, as I held these onion-paper letters in hand, that my grandfather was a follower of seasons, that he kept his eye on land and sky. I sensed already that there was a fundamental contingency to his life's work based on things beyond his ken—namely wind, weather, and Providence. If one of his letters had ever said, "Lord willing and the creek don't rise," it wouldn't have surprised me. Essentially, that's what they all said.

As for us who are city-dwellers, we are fond of the term *climate-controlled* and apply it to everything we can get our hands on—classrooms, cars, offices, homes, even storage facilities. Between attached garages at home and parking garages at work, scores of us don't set foot on the open earth for days at a time. When we do, our foot is as likely as not to rest on pavement, or at least cultivated grass. When is the last time you walked through weeds or wheat, mud or maize? Jesus and his disciples once cut through a wheat field on their way home from synagogue, providing a nice opportunity for a wheat-kernel snack on the go. We might be afraid to put such a strange thing in our mouths—after all, we don't really know where it came from.

In the city, save for the kids' soccer games, we don't let weather get in the way of much. Most of our jobs keep right on rolling through drought, rainfall, cold, heat, wind, and frost, never missing a beat. Even our sprinklers are indifferent to the weather, watering the lawn straight through a downpour. We could virtually ignore the seasons, and in many ways do, for all the immediate impact they have on our daily lives. Borrowing Old Jebb's question from Robert Penn Warren's *Blackberry Winter*, we could be saying "What June mean?" all through the year, filling in the month at hand. What does June mean? Or October? Or January? To us, not so much. To Jesus, it seemed, a great deal more.

Was Jesus attentive to the seasons for theological reasons? Did he understand that our lives and all of history are moving in a kind of linear cycle toward a divine purpose, a *telos*, a fulfillment? In such a view, seasons, signs, and cycles of time become mile markers of a sort, ushering us nearer the new creation, when God's kingdom will come in its fullness, God's will be done on earth as in heaven. Every year, every season, every moment ushers in new life, growth, surrender to that end. In *Fiddler on the Roof*, Tevya becomes philosophical about time's passage as he watches his daughters change overnight from little girls into grown women, marrying into families of their own: *Sunrise, sunset. Swiftly fly the years. One season following another, laden with happiness and tears.* Try singing that at *your* daughter's wedding, and you're likely to become philosophical too.

I have a sense that Jesus drew nature into his theological vision partly due to a holy regard he held for a natural realm that possessed its own logic and mystery. After all, a rancher-farmer's sense of contingency is not the exclusive possession of the rancher-farmer. So far as we know, Jesus did more hammering and nailing than herding and planting. Yet the carpenter-teacher was still able to follow the seasons.

One way in which we can direct our lives toward greater sufficiency and our lifestyles toward greater moderation is by paying greater attention to the natural world, its cycles and seasons, and our place within them. By developing our awareness of the sustaining forces of earth and sky that surround and enfold us, we are likely to walk more softly and understand more clearly our beholdenness to an environment that is in many ways shrouded in mystery, resplendent in change. We will grow to realize that "environment" is really a misnomer. Nature is not only our canopy, as though we carried out our detached human lives beneath some dissociated shell. Nature includes *us* as well. We are part and parcel of the whole earth in all its grit and glory.

This may sound funny, but one of the best places to learn to follow seasons may be the church house. There we learn to number our days, weeks, and months, waiting for Advent to bring us Christmas as the gardener waits for the winter rose to bloom, for Lent to bring us Easter as the farmer waits for a green-bladed sign that the spring wheat will make. There we wait for Ordinary Time to play out its ordinariness in the very way that growers from time immemorial have bridged intensely crowded harvest moments with days and weeks of nothing in particular—checking on this, shoring up that, mending a little fence, fixing the tractor, cleaning out cellar or hay loft toward the day of their resupply.

We wait in church the way we wait in nature, following seasons with a long-range hunger that is sure to be satisfied, but maybe not just yet. The time is now, and the kingdom of God has come near, Jesus said to a forward-leaning crowd on beginning his ministry (Mark 1:15). This has become the litany of our living through the Christian year. It's now. And it's near. His words still ring true, leaving us, for the time being, to regard the seasons between now and nearly—sunrise, sunset, harvest and planting, joy in the reaping, hope in the seed.

Chapter 24

Small Marble

Honey, life ain't nothing but strings.
Interviewee to Mary Pipher in *Another Country*

*I*n 1977 InterVarsity Press published a book about the world scene by a scholar named Ron Sider. The book was a searing critique of the economically developed world with regard to the hoarding of resources to the severe detriment of the remainder of the world's population. Sider laid responsibility for this gross global inequity squarely at the feet of people of faith. The book's title alone gives us plenty to lose sleep over: *Rich Christians in an Age of Hunger*.

What Sider asserts in his book is that there is no shortage of resources for feeding the world's population—only a shortage of interest. We simply don't want to be bothered. What would it mean for us to summon such an interest, to respond in meaningful ways to the world's astronomical human need? At the present time, thirty-five thousand children die each day of hunger-related causes. Meanwhile, Americans are growing obese in record numbers, as are our pets and landfills. We continue the time-honored practice of channeling massive volumes of edible grain toward beef production. Our kitchen disposals and trash compactors work overtime to process the food we throw away, and, in what has become an overnight sensation, we are now putting food in our gas tanks—converting corn to ethanol to help satisfy our gargantuan appetite for fuel.

The picture of such an extreme contrast between our hungry age and the rich Christians who live in it would be surreal were it not completely accurate. If there's any comfort in the fact, such gross disparity is not a new phenomenon. Jesus told the story of a man of robust appetite who feasted sumptuously while right outside his gate another man begged for the crumbs beneath his table and was roundly ignored. We may be living extravagantly while others are desperate for survival, but at least they are not right outside our gates like the poor man in Jesus' story. As Thomas Jefferson once put it, we are "kindly separated" by a wide sea from other nations and the threats they might pose. The aching poor of the developing world are thousands of miles away, far beyond our ability to do much for them, right?

Saudi astronaut Sultan Bin Salman al-Saud, part of an international team of astronauts who orbited the earth, gives us a more enlightened picture of things. He is quoted in Kevin W. Kelley's spectacular picture book, *The Home Planet*: "The first day or so we all pointed to our countries. The third or fourth day we were pointing to our continents. By the fifth day we were aware of only one Earth." The world has grown smaller through education, travel, international trade, cultural exchange, and the Internet, and the effective distance between people around the planet has been dramatically lessened. The world's poor—not to mention the poor of our own cities and neighborhoods—have come closer and closer to our awareness, closer and closer to our doorsteps, closer and closer to our overstocked pantries and second fridges. They are within a hand's reach of our sumptuous feasting. The only remaining question is whether they are capable of reaching our hearts. We have been "kindly separated" for centuries; can we now be "kindly joined" instead?

Recently, a performance artist pulled off one of the nuttiest stunts I've ever heard of. She tied herself to another person for a year. Fortunately, the other person agreed to the arrangement, and there were rules to be observed: no physical intimacy, no hurtful behaviors, and so on. You'll be relieved to learn that the cord binding them together was a generous six feet in length, far longer than it might have been. Even so, sleep schedules had to be shared, along with mealtimes, bathroom privileges, and, of course, going out alone in the night to ask the soul-searching question, *Why on earth am I doing this?* When the year was up, the artist was somber regarding the emotional and physical strenuousness of the experience. Her basic message was essentially a paraphrase of the sign you see when you're standing in line for the roller coaster at the amusement park: those with a history of heart problems should not ride this ride.

Imagine six and a half billion pieces of string, each about six feet in length, tying us all together—not for a year, for *life*. We would be forced to share everything, as though we were all *living on the same planet*. It is a scenario Kafka would have been proud to write. But is there a sense in which it describes our present reality?

In chatting with a friend at a party, we had one of those "It's a small world" discoveries, and she did the honors. "Small world," she said, to which I responded with a silly echo I first heard from a guy in South Texas. "Small marble," I said. Then she added a comment I wasn't expecting. "It's so small," she said, "you really need to behave." I've heard such things said of small towns, where everyone has their eye on everyone else's kids, or small campuses, where the administration can more or less monitor every student's shenanigans. But it was the first time I'd thought of that sort of accountability in a global context. So small, the world is, we really need to behave. We must come to our senses regarding the immorality of our immodest appetites and begin to moderate them.

What keeps us keeping on with our lifestyles of flagrant consumption when we know such practices are so destructive to

the earth and the millions who suffer hunger and other depri-
vation? Sin is the word we reserve for those ways we are and
things we do even when we know they hurt us, others, and
God. In one of his letters to the churches, Paul writes with
remarkable transparency: "I do not understand my own
actions. For I do not do what I want, but I do the very thing I
hate" (Romans 7:15). Can any of us relate? Paul's point is there
is not a one of us who *cannot* relate. We are all cut from the
same super-absorbent cloth as that first pair who wished to
bypass "enough" for "more."

What is our hope for deliverance from our super-absorbent
behaviors? Paul goes on to say, essentially, that Jesus the Christ is
the world's hope and our own. The same one who told the story
of the rich man and the poor man and the injustice of it all opened
wide his arms from where he hung on a cross and said, "Father,
forgive them; for they do not know what they are doing" (Luke
23:34). They do not know that they crucify one who loves them
more than any other. They do not know that as they neglect each
other they betray themselves. Father, forgive them, each and all,
for their appetites and longings are so closely intertwined they
have failed to distinguish between them. They think they crave
material security, but what they really desire is the trust that in
surrendering their fear of not having enough they will receive
from you assurance of a sort the world can never give.

As we stand before the compassionate figure of the crucified
Christ, a question pushes from our depths to the surface:
"What must we do?" The answer the church prefers to mum-
ble under its breath is "repent." Truth be told, the word gets a
bad rap. All in the world it means, from the original Greek,
metanoia, is "to change directions." Friends, I take that idea as
very good news. If we could never change directions, from our
first baby steps we'd have circled the globe several times by
now without having so much as left a note on the counter.
"Repent" is the best salve I know for another *re*-word, *regret*. If

I were to ask for a show of hands of those who would like the chance to heal some misunderstanding, take back an unkind word, respond to a need you once turned your back on, begin again in a relationship that has gone sour, I don't know how many hands would go up, but several would be reaching for a handkerchief.

A while ago I pulled up behind a guy in the sort of little car my wife, from first-hand experience, calls an econo-box. On the back of his car a bumper sticker read, "REPENT!" Strangely, there was no grim reaper beside the word, no scythe, no ball and chain. Instead, the letters of the word were bright and colorful, bouncing at angles like you see on a party invitation, with confetti and ticker tape all around. It was a joyful word, a festive word, a life-giving word. I didn't know the man from Adam, but I knew this—the guy in the econo-box was living large. I wanted to meet him, find out where he learned his vocabulary, hear what he knew about changing a life for the better. I wanted to follow him around for a while to see just what it means for repentance to be a party word rather than a punishment word. I was wishing the light would stay red long enough for me to dig in my trunk for a piece of string long enough to reach from my bumper to his. About six feet would have probably done the job.

John Oxenham wrote a hymn about reaching out to those who frighten us with their neediness. The hymn suggests that serving Christ through serving others is the "golden cord close binding humankind." Finding specific, tangible ways to reach out to those who are reaching out to us is how repentance begins to work its wonders in our lives. The cord that binds us, if we choose to reach across borders and boundaries to enter that matrix of blessing, is not the stuff of performance art, nor is it Kafka. It is true communion, and, for those who have known its tether, it is truly golden.

Chapter 25

The City and the Garden

> *. . . and the soil under the grass*
> *is dreaming of a young forest,*
> *and under the pavement the soil*
> *is dreaming of grass.*
> Wendell Berry

In the mid-1980s, a monumental shift occurred on the global demographic landscape. From that time forward, more of the world's population has inhabited urban areas than rural areas. The country mouse has moved to the city, but instead of swapping digs in keeping with the original story, the city mouse has decided to stay put, making for two city mice where there had been one. Repeat that scenario hundreds of millions of times, and you've arrived at the mid-1980s switch point. Before the shift, most humans on the planet (and mice, too, I would assume) lived out of a rural context, relating more easily to rural images, motifs, metaphors, and realities than to urban frames of reference. Since then, the reverse is true—most of us know sidewalks better than sunsets, overpasses better than okra plants.

We have become dual citizens—of a planet and of intra-planetary worlds of our own making known by the somewhat contradictory name of "urban environments." What does the shift from earth-dwellers to urban-dwellers mean for our world? And for us? How are we to integrate our understanding that we belong to the earth with the reality of being largely separated from the earth's crust by asphalt and cement—close kindred twice-removed?

After all, in earth's garden we were both created and called. The garden is the place of the fall, the curse, and the estrangement provision—the care and keeping God arranges for the errant Adam and Eve. Take away the nature/garden imagery from the sensuous Song of Solomon and you would have no song, and not much Solomon, either. The tiny mustard seed of Jesus' parable is embedded in the soil of a garden. In a garden a parade was organized for Jesus' entry into Jerusalem, and only days later, in that same garden, Jesus prayed in anguish before his arrest and crucifixion. Three days hence, Mary encountered the risen Christ in a dew-laden garden at early dawn, mistaking him, as you can understand, for the gardener. Earth's garden is the place of birth, decay, ecstasy, anguish, and resurrection.

In the introduction to a collection of gardening articles written by his wife, E. B. White recalls observing her, the autumn before her death, busy about the work of burying bulbs in her garden "under those dark skies in the dying October, calmly plotting the resurrection." Thomas Jefferson, up in years, weary from a lifetime of civil service to a patchwork nation, retired to his Virginia home and his beloved garden. "Though an old man," he wrote during those years, "I am but a young gardener." When I drove out to see Marshall Feldpausch the day after his oldest son was buried, having been the innocent victim of a fatal shooting, I found him in his vegetable garden, leaning against a plow, a long row yet ahead of him. He was quiet for a long while, then—I suppose by way of wanting to explain just why he was out working his garden during the mourning period—he finally said, "Anybody who's ever watched a garden grow would have to find a way to believe in God."

The garden of earth doesn't just *represent* life—it *conveys* life. It is the garden from which we draw food, flowers, and fragrance. It is where lovers meet in secret, laborers toil in broad daylight, summer's children play right up against the lavender hour where sunset and bedtime converge. It is the place within which we kindle longings both lofty and forbidden, witness love born and life renewed, insert our hands into dirt with a will, midwives to a birth. Romeo's entrancing words rise like flowers' fragrance from Juliet's garden—"See, how she leans her cheek upon her hand! O that I were a glove upon that hand, That I might touch that cheek!" *I smell the garden in your hair,* goes the lyric from the 1970s, and our very next breath retrieves the memory.

How are we to leave this resplendent garden life for the urban scene? Now that we are mostly here, is there a way in which we can find God, know birth, decay, ecstasy, anguish, and resurrection in the city? We call the Bible a good book in part because it possesses broad shoulders and is ample in the possibilities it offers for encountering God and living well "in all circumstances," as one of the Epistles puts it. It tends not so much to demand across the miles that the wandering pilgrim return home as create home *there*, reveal God just where the pilgrim is discovered trying to find their bearings. We call this peculiar behavior *incarnation*.

Given that tendency on the Bible's part to track and follow human endeavor, take a guess, then, what fairly modern phenomenon has won the attention and affinity of Scripture. You guessed it— the city. Whether by design or improvisation, we don't know and may never. In either case, cities emerge in the biblical narrative with a central role in holy history, not as second-rate substitutes for the earth's garden, but as places of spiritual sustenance and holy encounter in their own right. Jerusalem is home to the Temple, of course, and is, therefore, vested with singular status. "Our feet are standing within your gates, O Jerusalem," sing eager travelers on their way to the Temple for festival (Psalm 122:2). "All my springs are in you," others declare of that city (Psalm 87:7). In a most intriguing canticle, the city of Jerusalem, or Zion, becomes a metaphor for God, its exploration understood as essentially scoping out the divine: "Walk about Zion, go all around it, count its towers, consider well its ramparts; go through its citadels, that you may tell the next generation that this is God, our God forever and ever" (Psalm 48:12-14). Lest we assume Jerusalem has a corner on God's benevolence, Jeremiah corrects that assumption, charging the exiles who have been carted off to Babylon to "seek the welfare of the city . . . and pray to the LORD on its behalf" (Jeremiah 29:7).

The Gospels relate that the gossiping of the good news of Jesus in town was so electric that Jesus had to stick to the countryside for a while (Mark 1:45). Small wonder that, when reaching for a metaphor to describe what it meant for his disciples to be the light of the world, he settled on a city "built on a hill," unable to hide its light. Jesus' healing ministry took him into homes and synagogues as we might predict, but also, less predictably, into the urbane marketplace (Mark 6:56). Jesus healing in the marketplace? It is precisely where he wanted to be, for it was where the city's people were. "I must proclaim the good news . . . to the other *cities* also; for I was sent for this purpose" (Luke 4:43, emphasis mine). For the sake of what's coming next, remember our word for this: *incarnation.*

The final book of the Bible, Revelation, gives us a rare glimpse of the new creation, the time when God's purpose will have been fulfilled in the earthly and heavenly realms. The context for this new creation is . . . a city. And . . . a garden. That's right—both are present and accounted for *in one and the same vision:* "I saw the holy city . . . coming down out of heaven from God . . ." (Revelation 21:2). The city is then described in all its detail—including paved streets, gates, walls, foundations—all the usual trappings of a metropolitan scene. (Unlike those of the sumptuous diner in an earlier biblical story, these gates are never closed.) Then the weaving of city and garden begins: we're shown a river that flows through the middle of the city, and on either side of it, the tree of life, bearing fruit in abundance. We are told its leaves possess the power to heal nations.

In the culminating vision of the biblical narrative we're given a garden and a city conjoined, the marriage of farm and factory, soil and steel, green and gold. The God who walked the paradise garden in the cool of the evening and who was to be recognized in the ramparts and towers of Zion is present as ever, the light and lamp of the new garden city, city garden. The good earth is not compromised by the city, but draws it into its broad and generous folds, runs through it as a river to make the city glad, nourishes it with its fruit, mends it with its gift of healing leaves. Incarnation once again reveals itself in the sacred story, bringing heaven to earth, garden to city, God to us.

In the new creation vision, the city is a beholden place, deriving its brilliance from the presence of God, its refreshment from the river of life, its healing from the tree of life. Its prayers rise like incense, its towers like the evening sacrifice. The garden and the city, like hands braided in prayer, form a holy habitat of sustenance, healing, and worship before God the Creator, who has made all things well and has called all things good.

Grace Dancing

I danced in the morning when the world was begun . . .
Sydney Carter

*I know nothing, except what everyone knows—if there
when Grace dances, I should dance.*
W. H. Auden

A few years ago at the African American Museum in Dallas,
a special display featured hand-stitched quilts crafted by
African American women during the mid-nineteenth century.
On my visit one October day, the docent led me from quilt to
quilt, explaining the design, the background, the known details
of each particular item. One was patterned, another solid, a
third a patchwork of an old work shirt, britches, a flour sack.
Each looked time-worn and time-kept, just the way you want a
quilt to be—nicely broken in, but still sturdy enough for the
next winter's sleeping. I imagined those who had taken their
rest beneath these quilts after a long day's work and before
another and was reminded of the properties of grace.

She took me last to a quilt that was, to my notice, like all the
rest. It was an honest quilt with a simple pattern, faded into

131

comfort by over a century's use. Then she pointed out a minute feature I would have missed on my own: at a random spot on the quilt was a small sideways arrow, stitched in red. This quilt, she explained, was made for hanging on the clothesline of a sympathizer with the Underground Railroad. A fleeing slave passing by that place, breathless, would know from the embedded arrow which direction to go from there. Beneath the quilt provisions might be found, but the most important provision of all was that directional signal stitched like a whispered secret into the fabric of the quilt.

Of the properties of grace, that was one I had not considered, the one, I mean, that looks more like traveling papers than a hiding place. I prefer my quilts horizontal, warming me against the cold, rather than vertical, coded with arrows, sending me on further than I've already come. It occurred to me that in spite of my preferences the quilt of God's grace more than likely contains an arrow anyway. It warms me for the night, but at daybreak rustles me from my sleep and points the direction, by way of breakfast, toward freedom. Grace is free, Bonhoeffer once wrote, but it is not cheap. The demand it makes on us from the start and to the end is the surrendering up of our free-ranging wants to God's life-giving will.

The Bible's main words for God's will are something akin to longing, or desire. Next time you hear the phrase, "God's will for your life," instead of thinking "road map," think "yearning." God has a yearning, a longing for the world, for us. What is that longing? If we know our own truest longings, then we know God's: to see the world, and our lives within it, brought to wholeness; to see us, by the Spirit's power, summon the prevenient courage to say no to all that appears to be more but is really less. God yearns for us to *practice* saying no to these things, even if we don't quite mean it yet, and then gifts us with a divine yes, eased into the place left by what we've chosen to walk away from: yes to life, yes to the earth, yes to others, yes to God. Yes to every good and perfect gift that comes from above. Yes to the wealth that has nothing to do with money, the joy that has everything to do with self-giving, the shared life of work, rest, worship, and play that, sewn into a whole, becomes a life well–lived, a quilt stitched with an arrow.

If the patchwork of these pages has been something like that quilt, then I have offered all I know to give—a few scraps of work shirt, britches, flour sack. Then an arrow of sorts, stitched in, though not by me, something to settle and unsettle all at the same time, a challenge to turn from fear and misplaced consumption, and a promise that love and adequacy stand waiting in their place. As to how to choose love over fear, enough over more, questions remain for me just as I'm sure they do for you—I certainly haven't answered them all here. But there is that arrow, not so much a road map, more like the needle of a compass, pointing to what Thomas Bandy calls "the soul's true north," a land where our best efforts on a good day are enveloped in God's everyday grace.

Robert Penn Warren once wrote a poem about effort and grace, the tension between striving and surrender that defines our lives from cradle to grave and defines the life of all creation as well. The poem makes reference to Jacob, the rapscallion-saint, recalling his rough-and-tumble meeting with an angel one night by the Jabbok River (Genesis 32). The wrestling that ensued between the two like to have killed him, but instead, blessed him for life.

> *You dream that somewhere, somehow, you may embrace*
> *The world in its fullness and threat, and feel, like Jacob, at last*
> *The merciless grasp of unwordable grace . . .*

You'll notice how in the poem "embrace" rhymes with "grace," a thing also true in life. Our will, noble and stubborn, yearning for the good and also pushing against it, meets with the divine embrace, and is subsumed. The dreamer meets the Dreamer on the Dreamer's terms, and what we long for most deeply in our lives is given us, without benefit of mercy. If we are saved in the end by the things that ignore us—the Good Book in its unpretentious story of a modest God, parents in their unrelenting love, sacraments in their lifting and leveling, earth in its quiet keeping, quilts in their warmth and wending— then the final ignoring/saving gesture is the one that wrests from us all our doing, hoping, sinning, repenting, practicing, preaching, willing, and dreaming, and offers in its place something at once unwordable and all-sufficient: grace.

Over time, if our eyes are kind to us, grace is a reality we begin to see in all things—etched into the freedom trail, framed in the city lights, reflected in the rearview mirror, crosshatched into the forward landscape. Shakespeare knew there were "tongues in trees, books in running brooks, sermons in stones, and good in everything." Nowhere can we turn where God has not been first, or will not soon follow to find us out. God is ever with us; we are not alone.

We've made it to the yard of the perfect stranger whose clothesline holds a quilt stitched by another perfect stranger, whose hands are still getting used to freedom. We are tired from the long journey, but freedom is coming—we must press on. We sit for a borrowed moment in the shadow of the comforter to catch our breath and cool our brow before we travel on. Suddenly the wind stirs. The quilt sways gently in the breeze, the arrow still holding to true north. Now the quilt begins to look for all the world as though it is dancing—dancing, and for all the world. In such a moment, you and I both know there is only one thing to do: find a partner and join the dance.